the feminine way

DISCLAIMER: This is a work of nonfiction. Nonetheless, some of the names and identifying character traits of people featured in the stories herein have been changed in order to protect their identities (including stories used with the subject's full permission). Any resulting resemblance to persons either living or dead is entirely coincidental.

The publisher and Amy Natalie Pamensky make no representations or warranties of any kind with respect to this book or its contents, and assume no responsibility for errors, inaccuracies, omissions, or any other inconsistencies herein. The content of this book is for entertainment purposes only and is not intended to diagnose, treat, cure, or prevent any condition or disease, including mental health conditions. You understand that this book is not intended as a substitute for consultation with a licensed practitioner. The use of this book implies your acceptance of this disclaimer.

At the time of publication, the URLs displayed in this book refer to existing websites owned by Amy Natalie Pamensky and/or their affiliates. WorldChangers Media is not responsible for, nor should be deemed to endorse or recommend, these websites; nor is it responsible for any website content other than its own, or any content available on the internet not created by WorldChangers Media.

Paperback ISBN: 978-1-955811-54-5
E-book ISBN: 978-1-955811-55-2
LCCN: 2023916508

First paperback edition: November 2023

Cover design: Mila Book Covers / www.milabookcovers.com
Layout and typesetting: Bryna Haynes & Paul Baillie-Lane
Editors: Marie Schnoor & Bryna Haynes

Published by WorldChangers Media
PO Box 83, Foster, RI 02825
www.WorldChangers.Media

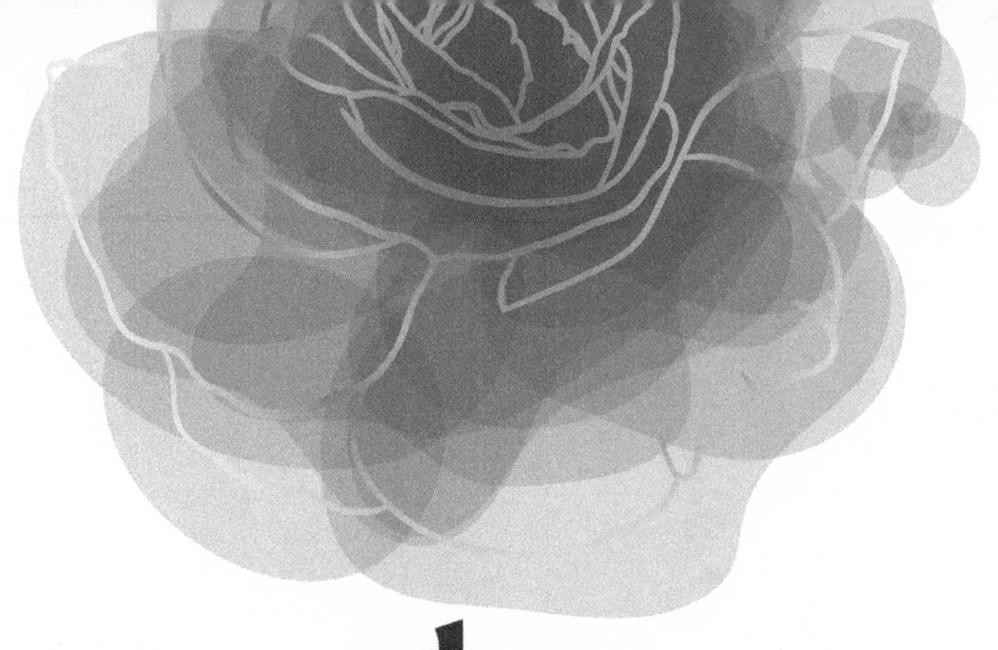

the feminine way

RECLAIM YOUR FEMININE ENERGY TO CREATE A LIFE OF PLEASURE, ALIVENESS, AND VITALITY

amy natalie pamensky

To all of the women who have come before me,
who walk beside me,
and who will come after me.

praise

"Awakening to our intuitive guidance and recognizing the spiritual awakening happening within us as women can no longer be ignored or suppressed. As creative, empowered, and connected feminine beings, we must align with and follow our own feminine ways to find a true sense of passion and purpose. *The Feminine Way* is the perfect avenue to assist all women on their empowered life path. I highly recommend this amazing book."

Christy Whitman, *New York Times* bestselling author of *The Art of Having It All: A Woman's Guide to Unlimited Abundance*

"*The Feminine Way* offers an excellent blueprint and step-by-step guide on how to soften, deepen, and empower yourself as a feminine being and leader. I recommend this to anyone looking to start the journey of exploring a new way of being and leading in the world that liberates us from our internalized patriarchy."

Nadia Munla, Embodiment Coach
and creator of Embody by Nadia™

If you've been searching, seeking, and yearning to live the life your Soul came here to experience, then *The Feminine Way* is the book for you. It's not only the ultimate guide to awakening your feminine energy, it's the resource that will offer you the transformations you've been waiting for. Amy Natalie Pamensky, through vulnerability, a decade of experience, and an embodiment perspective, is here to guide you back home to your Soul. I'm blown away by the magic and depth of this book: it's a permission slip to live a life of aligned joy, freedom, and pleasure.

Scout Sobel, CEO of Scout's Agency and
co-host of the Okay Sis podcast

"Amy's own embodiment of these feminine energies make her words come alive as she clearly and beautifully illuminates The Feminine Way. She gives readers permission to discover and awaken the deeper feminine energies within, not only for our own empowerment, freedom, and well-being but because these yearnings to actualize our own greater potential are, ultimately, the rising desire of life itself to live, love, heal, and awaken through us."

Johnny Blackburn, MA,
author and founder of Mystics

"From the depths of depression to ultimate freedom, *The Feminine Way* will take you on a heroic journey of reconnecting with your soul, on the deepest level, to cultivate a life that's rooted in truth, love, and authenticity. Get ready to dive deep, and open to a whole new magical version of yourself."

Tanya Lynn, author of *The Art of Leading Circle*
and founder of the Sistership Circle

"Amy's words are like a breath of fresh air, a sigh of relief, and an exhale for every woman across the world. This book is the reminder we all need that it's safe to slow down, it's okay to put your desires first, and that your intuition is your superpower."

Sam Altieri, speaker, podcast host, author,
women's leadership and business mentor

"*The Feminine Way* is an invitation and initiation for all women to remember their truest essence. Amy Natalie perfectly captures the essence of the feminine and offers to each of us a path forward to come home to our feminine wisdom. If you too are on the path of healing and self-discovery, trust your gut and pick up this book."

Dr. Cassandra Wilder, naturopath
and women's health expert

contents

Introduction

Finding My Feminine Way

I remember the exact moment I couldn't take it anymore.

I submerged my body deeper under the lukewarm water as the tears streamed down my face. Lost in my thoughts, I felt completely alone. My depression was the heaviest it had ever been, and I felt so hopeless and disconnected from myself. For over two years, my mind had been spinning in circles, overwhelmed and confused about how to move forward in my life. As I sat there, listening to the inner battle between my mind and my Soul, I still couldn't figure out the answer.

How was I going to get out of this dark and confusing place?

From the outside looking in, my life was perfect. I was married to a wonderful man, living in a beautiful three-bedroom house close to the beach, surrounded by loving family and friends, and running my own business. I couldn't understand how I could possibly feel so depressed when I seemed to be doing everything "right." Yet there I was, waking up every morning feeling anxiety pulsing through my chest before I'd even opened my eyes, dreading the day ahead.

On top of all this emotional turmoil, my physical health was in a downward spiral. Instead of admitting that something was fundamentally out of alignment, I kept blaming myself. The narrative that kept repeating in my mind was: "How can I be so ungrateful? What more can I want? What's wrong with me? Why can't I just be happy?"

As I sat there in the bath, my anxious thoughts once again turned to the biggest decision at play: my marriage.

My mind kept racing back and forth. "Should I stay? Should I leave?" And underneath these options, an even deeper question arose: "Can I trust myself?" This all-too-familiar inner dialogue continued to get louder. My Soul was screaming at me, but I wasn't ready to face the truth. My chest felt like it had a hundred pounds on top of it, my throat was clenching, and it seemed like the room was caving in. And yet the most concerning part was that I felt entirely empty inside.

I did my best to hide the pain I was experiencing. Even though I wore a pretty smile on my face for others to see, internally it felt like I was about to completely break. I was exhausted from pretending that everything was okay. The truth was that it wasn't okay. I wasn't okay.

I don't know what came over me next, but as I sat there cold and confused in the bathtub, there was an unfamiliar voice in my head saying, "You are not alone in this. There is a bigger plan for you. You don't have to figure this all out on your own."

A wave of relief instantly washed over me. I took a deep breath, and in that moment I felt a glimmer of hope.

After letting the words sink in, I lifted my chin, put my hand on my heart, and for the first time in my life, I looked up and started to pray. I didn't know exactly what to say, but I knew it was time to ask for guidance. I whispered out loud: "God, Universe, whoever is out there ... I need your help. I'm so tired. Please help me to get clarity; please guide me. I can't keep trying to figure this out on my own. Please show me a sign. Please tell me what to do next. I'm ready to listen."

I wiped away my tears, let out a long exhale, and waited for an answer.

How We Got Here

Perhaps at some point in your life you've had a similar moment: a time where it all came crashing in and you knew something had to change. If that hasn't happened yet, you may currently be feeling like something is "off," and there are big changes waiting on the horizon. Regardless of where you're at on this trajectory, it's important to know that these major crossroads usually don't happen overnight. They are a result of a series of decisions and experiences that occur over a period of months or years that bubble to the surface. Eventually, your deeper truth is revealed and you can no longer ignore your intuitive guidance. Something must change.

This kind of breaking point is commonly known as a quarter-life or mid-life crisis, yet from a spiritual lens these pivotal moments are referred to as spiritual awakenings. While the term "spiritual awakening" might sound intriguing, exciting, or even appealing, these awakening experiences can often be very unsettling, confusing, overwhelming, and even painful. However, it's through this awakening process that we're able to identify all of the thoughts, beliefs, and lifestyle factors that have not been serving us. In these pivotal moments, we're given the opportunity to redirect our path toward creating a life that's in alignment with our Soul.

But how do we actually do that?

You're in the right place to begin your exploration.

For centuries, Western society has significantly prioritized power, productivity, and financial status as metrics for success. As a consequence, it's been ingrained in our culture that the hyper-Masculine ways of constantly hustling, striving, and achieving are praised and valued, while the Feminine ways of nourishment, pleasure, relaxation, and rest are neglected and diminished. Over time, this imbalanced way of living has taken a toll on the mental, physical, spiritual, and emotional well-being of all of humanity. We've seen increasing rates of auto-immune conditions, mental health disorders, fertility issues, and burnout across all demographics, with women being the most highly affected. As a result, many of us are realizing that the old paradigm we've been living in—which has been heavily influenced by patriarchal and religious programming—is no longer a sustainable or viable way forward.

In the traditional model of Western society, we've subscribed to the ideology that the formula for success entails: going to a reputable college, getting a secure job, finding a partner to marry (before the age of thirty), buying a house, having 2.5 kids, climbing the success ladder, and saving for retirement. And while this has been the so-called "right way" to navigate life, this one-size-fits-all approach is clearly not the answer for everyone. If it were, people wouldn't be so burnt out, stressed, or sick, and they wouldn't wonder, "What's the point in all of this?" when they achieved the traditional success markers. So why is it that we have blindly been following the societal formula of hustling and achieving for success? For most people, up until now, it has been rooted in the survival mechanisms of feeling safe, secure, and accepted by others.

In an effort to live up to societal expectations and standards, we've lost touch with the Divine Feminine wisdom that was once woven into the fabric of everyday living. Over time, we've forgotten about the importance of connecting to nature, gathering in community, and enjoying the simple pleasures in life. We've been taught to ignore our intuition, to stuff down our emotions, and to conform to unrealistic beauty standards. It's no wonder that we're paying the price of dis-ease and dis-harmony in our bodies, in our minds, in nature, and in our society at large.

While there's nothing fundamentally wrong with the traditional markers of success, or with having a desire for safety and security, this cookie-cutter approach has not been effectively proven to deliver the results we think it's supposed to. Instead of experiencing happiness, fulfillment, and well-being, we have a population that feels sick, overwhelmed, and stressed out.

Even those of us who have followed the "success formula" and achieved the societal milestones are discovering that there's something missing from the equation. In my case, even though I followed the formula correctly by going to a good school, getting married, and buying a home, I found myself at the age of twenty-six feeling sick, depressed, and unfulfilled. Many of the clients I've worked with have reached the pinnacle of success in their careers. They've received fancy job titles along with financial abundance, yet they wonder why they feel so exhausted and disconnected. At some point, we start to question, "Is this really how it's supposed to be? There must be more to life than this!"

There *is* another way to live, and it's available to us all. This alternative path is for the awakening Souls who are discovering that the old paradigm is no longer working for them. The path that I'm presenting here looks and feels quite a bit different to the traditional pathway, and it requires you to "draw outside of the lines" of the societal guidelines and conditioning that you've learned up until now. This new way is guided by your Soul rather than your Ego, and it's rooted in your personal truth rather than what society has prescribed for you. It's designed to lead you out of dissatisfaction, disconnection, and burnout, and toward an extraordinary life in which you feel nourished, alive, and deeply connected. This is The Feminine Way: the path of trusting your intuition, listening to your body, and living in alignment with your truth.

As you open to receive the ancient wisdom of the Divine Feminine, you'll begin your healing journey to recover from the effects of the imbalanced Masculine—within yourself and in the world around you.

Our Feminine Awakening

For a moment, I want you to pause and picture what your life would be like if you had the ability to tap into your Feminine energy on a regular basis.

What would it be like if you were listening to your intuition, living as your authentic self, and feeling connected to your pleasure?

What would be different if you let yourself relax and enjoy the present moment instead of putting pressure on yourself to always be busy doing and achieving?

What would be different if you weren't stuck in your head all the time, overanalyzing and overthinking?

What would it be like if you allowed your emotions to flow through you and no longer felt trapped by anxiety, depression, or overwhelm?

What would be different if you felt comfortable and confident in your body and spent less time questioning your self-worth and seeking external validation?

Imagine how much energy this would free up on a daily basis, and how it would impact your relationships, health, career and overall happiness. What if I told you that you really could create a life of ease, flow, passion, and abundance, and that you didn't have to settle for anything less? What if all of this—and even more—was not only possible but within your reach, starting right this very minute?

If this sounds impossible, I want to reassure you that I felt the same way when I began my own Feminine awakening journey. If you'd have told me five years ago that I would be where I am (and who I am) today, I wouldn't have believed you. And yet, learning how to embody the principles of The Feminine Way has been the biggest catalyst for my personal healing and has transformed me into the woman I am today.

Six years ago, I was living a life that was governed by fear, control, self-criticism, and anxiety. Even though my Soul was guiding me to do things differently, I was too afraid to listen to it, for fear that everything would fall apart and I would mess up my whole life. I'd worked so hard to do things "right," so was I really going to let it all crumble? I'd followed the path to success, passed all of the milestones, and yet deep inside I still felt lost. For years I pushed that feeling aside, hiding it, covering it up, and denying it—until, at last, I let my truth overcome my fear and began to listen.

From the moment I surrendered, everything changed in a direction far better than I could have even imagined.

When I look back at the dreams and desires I wrote in my journal before I started living in The Feminine Way, I'm still in awe of how everything has come to fruition. As I allowed my intuition to guide me, my nutrition business quickly evolved into a personal transformation and spiritual development coaching business. I went from working in person with a few clients each week to serving thousands of women through my podcast, online courses, group coaching programs, events, and retreats. Within two years of fully stepping into my Soul Calling as a Women's Empowerment Coach and Feminine Embodiment Guide, my business income doubled, and I was finally attracting the Soul clients I knew deep down I was here to serve. Alongside the magnetism that was happening in my business, my health issues significantly improved, my energy increased, and my body shed the excess weight it'd been holding onto.

One of the greatest gifts I received during this time, as a result of following my heart, has been cultivating deep, intimate sisterhood relationships with like-minded women. For most of my life, I'd struggled in my relationships with other women. I always felt left out and never believed I could really be myself. I dreamed about having deep and supportive friendships with other women, but I just didn't know how to develop these connections. Within weeks of starting to live in my authentic truth, it was as if the friendships I always desired came out of nowhere. Today, I feel incredibly blessed to be surrounded by true, authentic sisterhood, and seriously don't know where I'd be today without the amazing women in my life.

The Feminine Way has changed every aspect of my life for the better. I've had the opportunity to travel the world, explore a deeply fulfilling and passionate romantic partnership, and continue to be blown away by the surprises that life brings my way. I followed my intuitive guidance, moved across the country, manifested a beautiful home, and connected with my Soul family in Asheville, North Carolina. There is nothing that brings me more joy than knowing that I'm living as my authentic self, actualizing my Soul's purpose, and creating a positive impact through doing work that I love.

My Feminine awakening journey has taught me how to surrender to the greater plan that the Universe has in store for me. My faith has guided me to a deeper understanding that I'm divinely supported as I continue to live in alignment with my Soul. As a result of the extraordinary transformation I've been through on my own journey, I've felt called to share this deep Feminine wisdom with as many women as possible.

This's why I know, deep in my bones, that this magical, mystical path of Feminine awakening is available for you, too. I know this because I've seen it happen—and the transformations I see in each and every one of my clients reaffirms how powerful tapping into Divine Feminine energy is. The women that I serve have experienced radical shifts in all areas of their lives, including their mental health, relationships, wealth, and an overall sense of aliveness. It's my strongest wish and belief that this can happen for you, too.

The Feminine Way will offer you a completely new perspective on every aspect of your life. It will reconnect you with the truth of who you are and realign you with the joy, abundance, pleasure, and ease you were born to experience in this lifetime. Throughout this journey, you will deepen your self-trust and confidence to make decisions that are authentic to your Soul. As you read, you may find that some of this information is not actually new to you; rather, it's a remembrance of a deeper truth that your Soul has known all along. The wisdom shared in these pages is designed to connect you with your Higher Self, nourish your spirit, and remind you of the infinite possibilities when you align with faith over fear.

Now, let me be clear: this way of living is not always filled with butterflies and rainbows. Challenges will still arise. You will have moments when fear tries to take over, and times where you question it all. The Feminine Way is not about having a perfect life or pretending that everything is amazing all the time. Instead, it's about having the confidence and trust in yourself to move through the challenges that come your way, and also having unshakable faith in the greater plan that the Universe has in store for you. This pathway still takes effort and commitment; however, in return for living in your truth, you get to experience synchronicities and magic along the way. And you get to experience the inner peace of knowing that you're living the life you were meant to live every day.

In this book, I will be guiding you on a journey to transform your inner landscape—your thoughts, beliefs, and energy—so that you can start to experience all of the healing benefits that The Feminine Way has to offer. The principles that you'll discover in these pages will support you to create the life you've always dreamed of: a life filled with ease, health, fulfillment, pleasure, and abundance.

How to Approach this Book

Before we go further into our exploration of The Feminine Way, I want to offer an introduction to the primary concept that we'll be focusing on throughout this book: the interplay between Masculine and Feminine energetics. At the most basic level, Masculine energy is rooted in logic, productivity, and doing, while Feminine energy is that of intuition, creativity, enjoyment, and replenishment.

If you're new to the concept of Masculine and Feminine energetics, these terms can feel confusing at first because they're also used to describe traditional male and female gender roles. However, while the names are the same, they have different meanings in this context. Around the world and throughout history, there are various methods of describing this interplay between Masculine and Feminine energies. In yogic philosophy, which is rooted in Hindu culture, Masculine and Feminine are personified as Shiva and Shakti. In Chinese philosophy, the duality of Yang and Yin, dark and light, represents Masculine and Feminine. In modern-day Conscious Relating teachings, I've seen these two energies referred to as Alpha (Masculine) and Omega (Feminine). Within each of these teachings, the main point to understand is that there are two dualistic, opposing yet complementary and integrated forces at play.

These two dualistic energies, Masculine and Feminine, exist within the greater Universal Field, as well as within every person regardless of their gender identity. More specifically, every woman has both Masculine and Feminine energy inside of them, and every man has both Masculine and Feminine energy inside of them. This is true for transgender and non-binary folks as well. The majority of this book focuses on inner union, which is the interplay between the Masculine and Feminine energies inside of you. As you create more harmony between these two energies within yourself, it will support you in creating more harmony in your intimate relationships, your relationship to your community, and your relationship to the earth.

There will be times throughout this book where we talk about these concepts as they relate to romantic relationships. To keep things simple, the terminology used when referring to the energetics at play will be shared through the lens of partnerships. To keep things universal, I've chosen to use the non-gendered pronoun "they" when referring to partners. Whether you identify as heterosexual, homosexual, bisexual, or otherwise, these concepts can (and do) apply for you. As I mentioned before, Masculine and Feminine energies are universal forces that exist within all living beings, the greater consciousness of humanity, and nature itself.

My invitation is for you to use your own discernment as you read through this book. Take what resonates and leave whatever does not. If any example or suggestion does not resonate with you, I invite you to swap it out and replace it with whatever feels most aligned and true for your unique circumstances.

Now that we've covered the primary concepts we'll be discussing throughout this book, let's dive into how you can get the most out of the teachings.

If up until now you've been approaching your spiritual development through a Masculine, hyper-productive, and goal-oriented lens, you may find yourself rushing through these pages so you can start making progress quickly and check this book off your reading list. Trust me, I've done that many times! However, it's my suggestion that you approach this book differently.

As you read, I invite you to slow down and give yourself permission to enjoy each step of this remembrance journey. What I've discovered on my own journey is that books, podcasts, and other educational media are far more effective when I take time for integration. While you'll gain a ton of value by intellectually learning about the concepts in this book, you'll only see results after you apply and embody the information. Throughout the chapters, you'll find guided practices to help you connect more deeply with the Feminine wisdom you're receiving. And at the end of each chapter, you'll find Soul Reflection journal prompts to support you in integrating the sacred concepts as they relate to your personal healing journey. You'll also find a bonus resources list with guided meditations and embodiment practices by going to www.amynatalieco.com/bookresources.

The process I'll be guiding you through in this book is based on my own Feminine awakening journey, my professional training as a Feminine Embodiment Guide, and the support that has been most effective for my Soul clients over the last six years.

Even though I'll be guiding you every step of the way, I want to remind you that you have your own inner guidance system, too. I invite you to use your intuition to guide you to whichever chapters and practices speak to you the most.

Here's an overview to guide you through the journey we're about to embark on together:

In Chapter One, we'll explore the shift that we've collectively been experiencing as we move into this New Age of the Feminine Rising. By gaining an understanding of this transformative New Age—also known as the Age of Aquarius—we'll paint a picture of the collective and individual future as we begin to come into alignment with The Feminine Way and find the path to heal these past wounds.

In Chapter Two, we'll go into more detail about the difference between Masculine and Feminine energies so you can be crystal clear on which energy you're operating from. We'll explore the dance between these two energies, how they support each other, and how to benefit from each of them. In this chapter, you'll also learn about a concept called "Energetic Agility" to become a master at transitioning from your Masculine to Feminine energy (and vice versa) based on what each moment calls for. And you'll discover the importance of leading with your Feminine energy to support your own healing journey, and to effectively contribute to the collective awakening that's underway.

In Chapters Three through Nine, we'll explore the Seven Feminine Codes that will guide you to deeper Soul alignment, abundance, health, and fulfillment. A "code" is similar to a principle, concept, or a lesson that's designed to unlock ancient wisdom, deeper healing, and inspiring possibilities that are accessible to you in this lifetime. Each Feminine Code has its own energetic frequency that you can consciously choose to receive and infuse into your life if it feels resonant and supportive for you. Here's an overview of the Seven Feminine Codes we'll be exploring together:

- Feminine Code #1: Deepening Devotion
- Feminine Code #2: Awakening Intuition
- Feminine Code #3: Emotional Alchemy
- Feminine Code #4: Prioritizing Pleasure
- Feminine Code #5: Soul Calling
- Feminine Code #6: Cyclical Living
- Feminine Code #7: Feminine Embodiment

Once we've covered all seven of the Feminine Codes, we'll learn how to integrate and implement The Feminine Way into your life in Chapter Ten. In this chapter, we'll review ways to build in the support and accountability necessary to maintain the new ways of being that you've been practicing throughout this journey. I'll give you the tools and resources to make sure this new way of living is sustainable as you move forward on your spiritual and personal evolution.

In Chapter Eleven, we'll explore the bigger picture of how your individual commitment of devotion to The Feminine

Way will create a greater impact on your relationships, your community, and on a larger global level as well. This is where we'll activate your role as a Divine Feminine leader who's here to create positive change in the world.

Regardless of where you're currently at in your own personal exploration of Feminine energy, I want you to know that you're exactly where you're supposed to be. You picked up this book at this specific time on your journey for a reason. The wisdom that's shared in these pages is designed to meet you where you are and expand you into your next level of transformation and growth. Everything you've learned up until this point has prepared you to receive the messages contained in this book. You're always in the right place at the right time, and it's no accident that this book found you at this point in your journey.

So, what do you say, love? Shall we get started?

"Every woman who heals herself helps heal all the women who came before her and all those who will come after."

Dr. Christiane Northrup

chapter one

The Feminine Rising

My eyes were wide open, but it was pitch black all around me. Underneath the warm, heavy blanket, my heart was beating out of my chest. I gasped for a deeper breath as the anxiety continued to rise. Turning to my phone, the backlight illuminated, the clock read 4:00 a.m. "Shit! Not again." I lay in stillness for a few minutes, listening to the slow, shallow breathing of my husband and my eight-month-old puppy in the background. Being careful not to wake anyone, I slid out of bed and tiptoed down the hallway into the guest room. Alone in the early hours of the morning, I opened the closet door, pulled out my round, turquoise meditation pillow, and placed it in the center of the room.

While I'd tried to start a morning meditation practice several times before, I'd never been successful at showing up consistently. Yet as the anxiety continued to wake me each morning, it felt as though I literally didn't have a choice. My Soul was screaming at me, desperately trying to get my attention. So there I was, doing my best to listen. Sitting up tall, feeling the soft yet firm cushion beneath me, I closed my eyes, put my hand on my heart, and focused on slowing down my breath.

As I sat there breathing and listening to a guided meditation, my thoughts were racing a million miles an hour, contemplating if I could really follow through with filing for a divorce. Even though my decision was clear, I couldn't stop thinking about how my choice would impact everyone else in my life. My parents. His parents. Our families. Our community. Our friends. Him.

The hardest part to reconcile was that there was nothing specifically wrong in our marriage. We didn't fight; in fact, we didn't even argue. We were close friends and had so many people who supported our relationship. Logically, leaving my marriage made absolutely no sense. But that voice inside of me kept getting louder, and I couldn't deny it anymore. I was unhappy. The Soul connection and intimacy that I deeply yearned for was not accessible in our relationship. At this point, I'd tried everything I possibly could to convince myself to stay. I drove myself crazy trying to ignore my inner voice, to suppress Her, to silence the truth that was burning inside of me.

As I sat in meditation, a question popped into my awareness, seemingly out of nowhere: "Are you going to keep trying to make everyone else happy, or are you going to choose your own happiness?"

At that moment, I realized I couldn't keep living a lie. Even though it felt selfish to choose my own happiness at the risk of hurting others, I ultimately knew that being inauthentic was not serving anyone. As I sat with this realization, I took out my journal and wrote an oath to myself. I made a promise that no matter how other people responded to my decision to end my marriage, I would stay true to myself and put my happiness first. For the first time in my life, I was willing to risk everything in order to prioritize my mental and physical well-being.

I got up from my meditation pillow and slid back into bed. At this point, my husband was awake, and I sensed that he knew something was off. He asked if everything was okay, and even though I'd planned to wait a few weeks to tell him, I couldn't hold it back any longer. It was by far the hardest conversation I've ever had, telling the person I cared about deeply and who'd been my best friend for the past five years that we weren't going to pursue the shared dream we once had together.

The weeks that followed were a blur. I experienced all of the emotions you could imagine: grief, sadness, guilt, shame, and a significant amount of relief. Even though the life and identity I'd built was completely crumbling around me, there was a deep inner knowing that I'd made the right decision. It felt like a huge exhale to release the weight of all the confusion, indecision, and resistance that I'd been carrying in my mind and in my body.

This life-altering decision to leave my marriage was far more than just a decision to end a relationship. This decision marked the completion of living my life according to what society, religion, and my parents had wanted for me, and the beginning of living a life that was authentic and true to my Soul. From the moment I took this huge leap of faith, I started to experience incredible miracles on a daily basis. It was as though the Universe had been waiting for me to listen to my truth and was sending me little reminders that everything was going to be okay.

Within weeks of making my decision, my health symptoms started to subside. The extra weight I'd been carrying on my body started to melt away, my skin was glowing, and my digestive symptoms significantly improved. For the first time ever, I felt a sense of peace, joy, and clarity that lasted for more than just a fleeting moment. Even as challenges and grief would arise, I realized that I was able to meet myself with a new sense of compassion and love, which helped me to process my emotions much faster than before. As the weeks went on, I miraculously started making friends with like-minded women, attracting new Soul clients, and was presented with opportunities I'd been dreaming about.

Simultaneously, while I was experiencing my own spiritual awakening, I started to recognize that there was a larger awakening happening in the collective. As my eyes opened to this new reality and way of living, I saw other women around me awakening as well. I could tell how hungry women were for this information and started to integrate the lessons I was learning into my coaching practice. As my clients implemented this Feminine wisdom into their lives, it was incredibly rewarding to see that they started experiencing life-changing results as well. These are the exact principles and tools I'll be guiding you through in this book to help you take the leap out of the old paradigm and start living in The Feminine Way.

Embracing the New Age

We're living in a time of rapid change and evolution of human consciousness. Spiritual teachers, astrologers, sages, and mystics have referred to this time as "The Great Awakening," "The Rising Feminine," and "The Age of Aquarius." More and more people are waking up to the truth that there must be a different way to live. As a collective, we're shifting out of the Masculine-dominant, patriarchal way of operating and moving into an era that will bring the Divine Feminine and the Divine Masculine back into balance.

According to astrology, we're moving out of the Piscean Age and into the Aquarian Age. This major astrological shift only happens every 2,000–2,160 years. It may not surprise you that the characteristics of the Piscean Age, which has been influencing society for the past 2,000 or so years, are rooted in consumerism, materialism, money, and power. This, in turn, has led to a culture that is addicted to the nine-to-five hustle, always staying busy, and obsessed with consumption. As a result, it's common to feel like you are never doing enough—and, by extension, that *you* are never enough.

In contrast, the Aquarian Age has quite a different approach and energy. This new era that we've recently entered is characterized by creativity, intellect, community, and collaboration. This age is about valuing innovation, individuality, and working together to create positive change. On a practical level, this looks like a world where it's normal to pursue a career path that's aligned with your natural talents and skills. Rather than obsessing about how productive you are and how many hours you work, the focus is on doing things that you're passionate about and creating a schedule that honors your natural cycles of energy. As you contribute your gifts to the world, you no longer have to figure it all out on your own. Instead, you're surrounded by a supportive community of like-minded people where you feel celebrated for who you are and respected for your creations and authentic expression.

While the old paradigm has taught women that putting ourselves first is selfish, the new paradigm celebrates us for prioritizing ourselves, because it's only from this place that we can authentically (and sustainably) contribute our love, energy, and gifts to the collective. Gone are the days when we abandoned ourselves and sacrificed our needs so that we could be everything for everyone at all times. When we're exhausted, nobody receives the best version of us. The New Age being birthed is reliant upon you focusing on your inner healing and showing up as your most powerful, authentic self.

As more and more people awaken to these new ways of being, feel the pull of their Higher Selves, and question the current paradigm, it's evident that the Aquarian Age is well underway. People are waking up, no longer content to go through life on autopilot and continue doing things the way they've always been done. While there have been many advances in technology, science, and finance, the old way has brought us to where we are now: burnt out, overwhelmed, empty, hollow, and eternally chasing the next external marker of success. And for what?

While it's true that external things like getting the next job promotion, making more money, and having a bigger house can be great, none of them will ever lead to the kind of Soul-deep satisfaction that comes from living in authentic alignment with your truest self. However, this doesn't mean that you're forced to choose between financial success or living a Soul-led life. You don't need to "sell your Soul" for financial abundance, nor do you have to abandon your goals of stability and security in order to live in nature with no possessions at all. Within this new paradigm, it's possible to be spiritually fulfilled and financially successful.

For mainstream individuals, these ideas may seem radical, even revolutionary. They're certainly disruptive. But the truth is, these ideas aren't new. For decades, there's been talk about the New Earth and the New Age within spiritual communities. This vision for the future is one rooted in love, truth, and connection. At times, when we let the chaos and confusion of our global landscape overwhelm us, it can feel hard to believe this new paradigm is even possible—especially when our government, healthcare, education, and financial systems are growing less and less stable, and that the safety and security they've promised is no more than an illusion. People are beginning to recognize that the foundations of these formerly trusted systems are actually rooted in fear, greed, and power. In the New Age, anything not rooted in love and truth will not survive, which is why it's not surprising that the faults in these systems are starting to surface.

And yet, while these systems are beginning to crumble, I look around at the incredible healing that's happening on both an individual and collective level. It's undeniable that there's great change upon us. As with any great change, we must be willing to release the old to create space for something new to be birthed.

Times of change often bring up feelings of uncertainty and discomfort in our nervous systems. This happens because the human Ego loves predictability, and it likes for everything to stay the same in order for us to feel safe from potential danger. Any time we try to step outside of our comfort zone, it's normal to experience a physiological response of fear and anxiety because our Ego is trying to protect us from the unknown. However, in these moments we have a choice: we can hold onto the past, or we can embrace the new and move forward from a place of trust and faith. In the short term, it can feel terrifying to take the leap and follow a new direction. (I know this feeling all too well!) But in the long term, it's far more painful to resist the changes we're being called to make. Living in a place of fear and not honoring our truth not only impacts us as individuals, but also impacts the whole ecosystem of people around us.

Envisioning the New Paradigm

As the old paradigm falls away, it can be helpful for your mind to connect with the vision of what the emerging New Age looks like. Let me paint a picture for you.

The new paradigm is about bringing the Masculine and Feminine energies back into balance within yourself and within the collective. It's about getting out of your head and coming back into your heart. It's about releasing control and inviting more trust, faith, and openness into your life. It's about surrendering to a greater plan. It's a time to let your intuition lead the way, to listen to your truth, and to show up courageously as your authentic self.

The new paradigm is about acknowledging and celebrating your unique Soul gifts, generously sharing them with others, and being divinely compensated in return. In this new reality, we're being called to source our validation and worth from within rather than seeking approval from others, and to express ourselves unapologetically. With this comes a remembrance of slowing down, connecting, and tuning in to the Divine Intelligence that exists within us and within nature. It's about reconnecting to Mother Earth, healing our planet, and honoring the natural cycles of life while simultaneously honoring our own cyclical nature and tuning in to the wisdom of our bodies.

The new paradigm is about collaboration over competition. It's about coming together in sisterhood to support, inspire, and lift each other up. This is the time to reignite your pleasure, your aliveness, your creativity, and your joy. This is exactly why your Soul chose to be here at this time in history, to be a Feminine leader and agent for positive change and healing. As such, you get to play and explore your own unique expression of the Divine Feminine. This is an opportunity for each of us to peel off the masks that we've been wearing in order to fit in, and instead be unapologetic in our aliveness, joy, pleasure, and self-expression.

Most importantly, amidst the vast and global changes that this new paradigm brings, the greatest journey is one of returning. Many of my clients, colleagues, and Soul sisters have described the shift into the new paradigm as a journey of "coming home to yourself"—not the you that society wanted you to be, but the authentic, powerful, joyful version of you who's been waiting all this time to rise.

How Did We Get Here?

Before we can evolve into this new paradigm, it's important to understand how we got here in the first place.

For thousands of years, the Divine Feminine has been neglected, caged, suppressed, and silenced. Throughout history we can witness a pattern that weaves its way through religious and societal institutions, a legacy of patriarchal ideology. From the very first woman in the Bible, Eve, being portrayed as untrustworthy and irresponsible for eating the fruit of the forbidden tree, to the centuries of persecution that witches, healers, mystics, and intuitives have endured, the Feminine has been undermined and diminished.

At the root of this oppression has always been a fear that the Divine Feminine is a threat to the powers that be. When we connect with the magnitude that the Divine Feminine holds, it's not surprising that the patriarchy has done whatever it takes to diminish Her. This sense of unapologetic aliveness, of deep and profound intuition, and magnetic pleasure and eros, runs contrary to the power structures that are at the foundation of patriarchal and capitalist ideologies.

In an attempt to control and reduce the power that the Divine Feminine holds, the patriarchy has turned women away from their true nature, demanding that women modify their behavior, appearance, and identity to fit into the mold of the "Good Girl." We as women have given up our power to be acceptable according to societal standards as a way to protect ourselves and to survive.

In her book, *Break the Good Girl Myth*, author Majo Molfino explains that "the good girl is [the] domesticated part of ourselves that has been tamed and trained by this system over our entire lifetime and perhaps even multiple generations of women in our families. When we embody her, we play it safe, hold back our voices, and don't share our true gifts with the world." She further explains that the patriarchy "is not a single individual or group of people (i.e., 'all men'). It's synonymous with dominant culture, which means it trickles down invisibly into our communities and subcultures."[1]

Most importantly, each of us needs to understand that the patriarchy is not something "out there." It lives within each and every one of us. We've inherited the cultural norms and social programming that directly and indirectly says that Feminine qualities are not as valuable as Masculine qualities.

Because we've absorbed this information, we subconsciously (or sometimes even consciously) behave in ways to overcome these discrepancies, to prove our worth, and to strive for equality with men. Based on these underlying, patriarchal social guidelines that we've adopted, we've learned to modify our behavior and personalities to conform to these imbalanced societal norms. For example, in Western culture, the Feminine gifts of intuition, sensuality, and emotionality are often perceived as weak and inferior to the Masculine qualities of logic, assertiveness, and directness. This affects every single one of us.

While women suffer under the effects of both external patriarchal systems as well as internalized patriarchy, men aren't immune to the toxic effects of the patriarchy either. Although the patriarchal framework seems to benefit men at the expense of women, everyone loses when the Feminine is suppressed. When women are taught to suppress their Feminine qualities in order to get ahead in the fiercely competitive world, they often feel depleted, as if they are pulled in opposing directions. They dare not give in to their intuition, their warmth, their nurturing, or their emotions, lest they be perceived as weak, emotional, or out of control. Similarly, men are taught from a very young age that to display any Feminine qualities is inferior and shameful, and that displaying such qualities undermines and interferes with the Masculine, linear, achievement- and logic-focused framework under which our society operates. They learn to suppress their Feminine qualities in order to live up to the "manly" standard, to avoid being called "weak," "soft" or "girly"—but emotions are intrinsic to the human experience. Emotions themselves are not dangerous, but when men suppress them, they too experience extreme distress that can lead to dangerous, even deadly, results.

In light of all this, it's no wonder that we're afraid to outwardly express our Feminine qualities. And while everyone suffers under patriarchal conditioning, there's a lasting legacy of destruction and suppression that women have inherited in today's world. It wasn't so long ago that women were burned at the stake for expressing their Feminine power, sharing their spiritual gifts, and expressing their sacred sensuality. The mental health epidemic is nothing new, but in decades past, "unstable" or "hysterical" women were sent away, institutionalized, or given various horrific "treatments" to make them behave the way society wanted them to. Even with the gains toward equality and equal representation, the Feminine continues to be suppressed in corporate workspaces, religious communities, and social settings, where women who express their boundaries or speak their truth are labeled as weak, dramatic, bitchy, or selfish.

As a result, we've become disempowered and terrified to embrace our Feminine qualities for fear of being harmed, outcast, or feeling "less than." Over time, the pain of suppressing our true nature creates a significant impact on our mental and physical well-being. It's exhausting to modify our authentic selves in an attempt to be the version of ourselves that society expects. Our Divine Feminine essence is powerful, natural, and deeply ingrained within us. When we suppress our emotions, our intuition, our power—when we suppress any and all of the Feminine qualities—they don't just go away. That energy gets expressed in unhealthy and often harmful ways.

And She Rises

Even when we do our best to perform to unrealistic Masculine standards, it never seems to be enough. It's no wonder that we try to numb out the pain by turning to any number of coping mechanisms that soothe us for a time but can't really fix anything. From alcohol abuse to overusing prescription pills or other substances, to other forms of numbing and avoiding like shopping, emotional eating, browsing online for hours at a time, an overdependence on social media, or even mindless TV watching, we distract ourselves from the truth that we don't feel at home in ourselves. However, none of these coping mechanisms will help because none of them truly get to the heart of the problem.

As the collective consciousness rises, these outdated standards and viewpoints are starting to shift. There has been tremendous progress over the past couple of decades where thousands of women have emerged out of the "spiritual closet" to challenge the status quo of how we're expected to look, act, and behave. We've seen a resurgence of the Divine Feminine, which is evident through the rise in modern spiritual teachers, priestesses, witches, and healers who are courageously showing up to share their truth and spiritual healing gifts, along with many other women who are awakening to their truth and are actively seeking how to infuse more Feminine energy and spiritual healing into their lives. Now is the time to continue identifying and unlearning your own misconceptions about the Feminine so that you can embrace your true, empowered Feminine expression.

The ultimate purpose of the Feminine awakening is to bring us back into harmony with both the Divine Masculine and Divine Feminine for greater peace, healing, and freedom. It's for this reason that the time we're living in is referred to as "The Feminine Rising." The Feminine is not only rising in women, it's an energy and consciousness that's rising throughout the collective, within individuals and in society as a whole.

The Feminine Way is here to guide you to your own inner equilibrium of Masculine and Feminine energies, which in turn will support you in bringing this energetic harmony into your relationships, your family, your community, your life's work, and society at large. Together, we will walk the path of The Feminine Way to course correct and heal from the damage that's been caused as a result of the old paradigm.

Misconceptions of the Feminine

When you hear the word "Feminine," certain images or beliefs will automatically come to mind whether you're consciously aware of them or not. Generally speaking, many of the preconceptions we've held about the Feminine up until now are a result of the collective "wounded Feminine" expression, which is what happens when we give away our power and let down our boundaries. When we carry shame around our emotions, silence our voices, and repress our sexuality, we can become passive, manipulative, controlling, dramatic, or selfish.

Alternatively, when the Divine Feminine is supported, encouraged, and celebrated, and when we're empowered to relate to our Feminine attributes without any shame or judgment, the true nature of the Feminine is free to express itself in more empowered, inspiring, and responsible ways.

As we begin to individually and collectively unlearn the toxic Masculine programming that we've been exposed to, we'll be able to experience the positive healing aspects that the Divine Feminine has to offer in bringing more harmony, health, and vitality into our lives.

Divine Femininity is powerful beyond measure. More than just powerful: it's essential. Making this shift and opening up to meet Her means we can begin to heal the wounds caused by the patriarchy and reclaim true physical, energetic, and emotional balance in our lives.

- ***Wounded Feminine:*** Passive, overwhelmed, indecisive, dramatic, codependent, docile, overreactive, manipulative, controlling, judgmental, submissive.
- ***Empowered Feminine:*** Loving, courageous, brave, fierce, nurturing, intuitive, empathic, compassionate, creative, passionate, magnetic.

Misconceptions of the Masculine

In a culture that has been obsessed with power, dominance, and control for centuries, both men and women have adapted an unhealthy relationship with Masculine energy. When we relate to Masculine energy in an Egoic and unconscious way, it lends to disruptive behaviors that cause separation, destruction, and harm. Alternatively, through developing a healthy and trusting relationship with the Divine Masculine, we can create a powerful container for safety, trust, and growth.

- ***Wounded Masculine:*** Resentful, angry, controlling, overbearing, domineering, aggressive, overly competitive, sexist, violent.
- ***Empowered Masculine:*** Trustworthy, steady, grounded, present, integrous, gentle, leads by example, connected to emotions.

In recent years, we've seen a tremendous effort from conscious men to heal their toxic relationship with Masculine energy through individual and group work. We, as women, also have the opportunity to heal our own wounded relationship with the Masculine by healing our relationship with men, with religion, and with authority. As we come into right relationship with our own Masculine energy, we simultaneously allow the Divine Feminine to be supported and elevated. So, let's begin with deepening our understanding of what the Feminine is, in all Her complexity and power.

Different Flavors of the Feminine

The Feminine is not meant to fit in a pretty little box. There's no one specific way that you're supposed to look or act when you're connected to your Feminine energy. When we peel back the layers of toxic programming and expectations about how women are supposed to behave, we're left with a blank canvas for the true nature of the Feminine to reveal Herself.

The Feminine is ever-changing. She's a reflection of whatever feels authentic and true for you. One of the gifts of accessing your true Feminine nature is that you get to be your authentic self in any given moment. Rather than trying to look like you have it all put together or trying to act like someone you see on social media, connecting with your Feminine energy is about showing up exactly as you are.

At times, your inner Feminine may want to express Herself through being creative, sensual, loving, soft, and nurturing. Other times, your Feminine may want to express Her fierceness, rage, sadness, child-like wonder, or playful nature. Some days, your Feminine may want to be expressed through wearing long, flowy dresses, adorned with jewelry and glitter; other days, She might desire to show up in sexy lingerie, or sweatpants and a messy bun.

The best way to get to know your own unique expression of the Feminine is to do the inner work to release the misconceptions and programming you've been carrying, and to start connecting with what feels authentic for you. Connecting with your Feminine energy is less about trying to "do it right" and more about connecting to what feels good and true for you. You'll know you're connected to your Feminine energy based on how your body and your energy are feeling at any moment throughout your day. When you're living in alignment with your Feminine energy, you'll notice that you feel open, soft, connected, and alive. When you're living out of alignment with your Feminine energy, you'll notice that you feel stressed out, overwhelmed, contracted, and disconnected.

When you first start reconnecting with your Feminine energy, it can often feel uncomfortable and unpredictable. Especially if, like many women, you've been unconsciously hiding certain parts of your personality and your authentic expression, it can feel scary and messy to bring these aspects of you back online. For example, if you're used to pretending that everything is okay and not allowing others to see that you're experiencing emotions or challenges, it can feel vulnerable to be witnessed in your true feelings. Or perhaps you're not used to making decisions based on your intuition and you feel afraid that other people might view you as irresponsible or irrational when you share your desires and your vision. After operating in Masculine overdrive for so long, it makes sense that embracing more of your Feminine energy could feel like an uncomfortable edge.

However, in time, once you become more attuned to your relationship with your Feminine energy, these feelings will shift. Instead of feeling like you need to hide your emotions, you'll notice more closeness and intimacy in your relationships. Instead of feeling unproductive or lazy, you will recognize the importance of honoring your own cycles of rest and renewal. Instead of feeling as if you must rely on logic to navigate your life, you'll be able to let go of control and surrender into Divine Feminine flow. This is the ultimate goal of The Feminine Way: to help you nurture your Feminine essence, get out of Masculine overdrive, and gain the discernment and wisdom to approach life from a state of balance and harmony.

Answering the Call

Since you're reading this book right now, it's clear that you're feeling the call to deepen your connection with the Divine Feminine. Perhaps you've reached your own breaking point with feeling stressed, overwhelmed, and depleted. Or maybe you feel inspired to experience more pleasure, health, intimacy, and fulfillment in your life. Regardless of what's calling you forward, you're being asked to reconnect with the Divine Feminine for a reason—not only for your own personal well-being but also for the collective healing of humanity and our planet. As you deepen your relationship with the Divine Feminine within yourself, you'll create a ripple effect of healing and positive change all around you.

In the next chapter, we'll explore what it looks like to integrate the Masculine and Feminine energies inside of you so that you can infuse more harmony into every aspect of your life.

Soul Reflections

- What underlying fears do you have about incorporating more Feminine energy into your life?
- What misconceptions of the Feminine are you still holding onto within yourself and/or about others?
- What benefits do you see available by incorporating more Feminine energy into your life?

"There is a collective force rising up on the earth today, an energy of the reborn feminine ... This is a time of monumental shift, from the male dominance of human consciousness back to a balanced relationship between masculine and feminine."

Marianne Williamson

chapter two

Feminine and Masculine Dynamics

As I sat across the desk from my naturopathic doctor, sunlight streamed through the windows and a glimmer of hope arose in my chest. After years of experiencing chronic digestive problems, hormone imbalances, and more recent symptoms of extreme fatigue and unexplained weight gain, I was determined to get to the root cause of my health issues.

My doctor laid out my lab test results in front of me. "According to your hormone panel, it shows that your body is in a significant stress response and your cortisol levels are completely out of balance." If I kept operating at these higher stress levels, she informed me, my body would continue to be in an inflammatory state, and it would take a long time for my digestion to heal.

Before this point in my life, I'd been a relatively healthy young adult. Growing up as a dancer and being an athlete throughout high school and college set me up for a healthy trajectory. Yet within the span of a few years, my physical health symptoms went from being minor irritations to daily distractions and discomforts. My body became hypersensitive to many of my favorite foods; I felt bloated and uncomfortable most of the time, and my sugar cravings were at an all-time high. Even with consistent exercise and eating a healthy, nutritious diet, my body was holding onto excess weight, and I felt exhausted for most of the day. Eventually I got sick and tired of being sick and tired, and started searching for some answers.

Receiving the results from my lab tests was equally relieving and disappointing at the same time. My doctor recommended several supplements and lifestyle changes to reduce my stress levels. Some of the main suggestions were to manage my emotional stress, focus on getting more sleep, and take a break from the HIIT (high-intensity interval training) workouts I loved so much. Hearing these recommendations felt like a hit to my Ego, considering that so much of my identity was wrapped up in being an athlete and a highly ambitious person.

The first time I went for a walk instead of my usual run, I remember thinking how lame it was. I was convinced that this couldn't possibly be "real" exercise. The idea of slowing down and resting was completely foreign to me because I was addicted to being active and productive. Yet I was determined to feel better and continued to follow the protocol as best as I could. Within less than a month of scaling back my exercise and allowing my body to rest, I was surprised to see that the inflammation in my body had started to decrease. Even though

I was doing significantly less intense workouts, my clothes were fitting better and my energy was coming back online.

These health improvements inspired me to learn more about what was at play on an energetic and spiritual level, which is when I first discovered the concept of Masculine and Feminine energies. Very quickly, I realized that not only was I operating in Masculine overdrive with my nutrition and exercise, but that this pattern of overdoing was showing up in my relationship, in my business, and in my daily lifestyle. Having awareness of this imbalance and learning about this new framework completely changed everything for me. It felt empowering to have some answers about why the passion had died in my relationship, why it felt so challenging to grow my business, and why I felt an undercurrent of stress throughout my everyday life.

After five years of studying Masculine and Feminine energetics, implementing this body of work into my life, and going through a ton of trial and error, I'm finally in a place where I've been able to embody the integration of the Divine Masculine and Divine Feminine in all areas of my life. As a result of this work, my health has dramatically improved, I experience more intimacy and passion in my romantic relationship, and I feel more pleasure and joy in my life on a daily basis.

The good news is that it doesn't need to take you five years to figure out how to invite more Feminine energy into your life. In the upcoming chapters, I'll guide you through a clear process using the Seven Feminine Codes that will empower you to create more harmony between your own Masculine and Feminine energies. As you move through your journey, it's going to take awareness and daily devotion to be able to embody this new way of being. At first it will likely feel messy, and it may even feel like you're taking two steps forward and one step backward. But with persistence and practice, you'll start to experience the transformation within yourself and directly see the benefits reflected in the world around you.

In order to set the foundation for our journey together, we're going to take a deeper look at how to identify the imbalances between your Masculine and Feminine energies, and gain an understanding of what it looks (and feels) like when you've successfully embodied the synergy between them.

Energy in Harmony

Masculine and Feminine energies are meant to work together in harmony. Without both of these complementary energies, life itself wouldn't exist. However, in our modern world, because Masculine energy has been prioritized and glorified, we've forgotten about the sacred gifts that the Feminine has to offer, which has led to an imbalanced and Masculine-dominant way of living. As the Feminine rises in the collective, we're learning how essential it is to infuse more Feminine energy into our lives so that we can come back into harmony within ourselves, our relationships, our communities, and with the earth.

Nature is one of our greatest teachers when it comes to understanding the way that Masculine and Feminine energies are designed to work together in union. For example, when we look at a river, the outside structure of the riverbed offers Masculine support and direction for the Feminine flow of the water to move through. Without the riverbed, the water would go everywhere, but without the water, the bed would be dry and lifeless. When the two energies work together, the water can flow and bring life to humans, animals, and plants.

Similarly, when we look at trees, we can see the tree trunk is solid, rooted, and grounded, while the branches and the leaves are constantly flowing and evolving, providing us with adequate shade and nourishment. In both of these examples, Divine Masculine energy is here to provide structure and protection while the Divine Feminine is here to offer flow and nourishment.

The same is true for us as humans with regard to the balance of our own internal energies. For those of us who've been living in Masculine overdrive, we already know what the effects of this imbalance of energies is; without the Feminine, we become physically depleted and energetically malnourished. But the same is true on the opposite extreme, too. Without being able to tap into Masculine structure, our Feminine energy would become chaotic, ungrounded, and stagnant. We would be lost in the clouds, and we wouldn't get anything done.

The journey toward creating inner union between your Masculine and Feminine energies is unique to each individual. As you begin to explore these ideas of Masculine and Feminine energies, you may feel called to slowly implement new ways of being into your everyday life, such as incorporating a daily embodiment practice or creating space for your creative passions and hobbies. On the other hand, if you're completely burnt out and depleted, you might need to swing all the way into a Feminine-dominant state in order to replenish and nourish your energy before you can come back into a healthy equilibrium. This might look like taking time off work, taking a break from intense exercise, or reducing the frequency of your social engagements to give yourself space for deeper healing and recovery. The journey is yours, and you get to decide what your path is going to look like. Eventually, through the process of The Feminine Way and the Seven Feminine Codes you'll be learning in the coming chapters, you'll find the equilibrium that's right for you.

Let's dive deeper into the fundamentals of Masculine and Feminine energies.

Masculine Energy

In simple terms, Masculine energy can be thought of as "doing" mode. It's logical, linear, and focused—the energy of taking action toward a goal, or completing the tasks on your to-do list. When you're operating in your Masculine energy, you'll find that the wheels in your mind are spinning and there's a lot of mental focus happening. The Masculine is the intellectual part of you that likes to learn new things and figure out the solution to problems. It's also the part of you that needs organization and structure to stay grounded and productive.

One of the most powerful qualities of the Masculine is that it helps you to focus on your purpose and bring your ideas to fruition. You can use your Masculine energy to set inspiring goals and to have the inner discipline to follow through on them. Your Masculine energy helps you to set clear boundaries with your time and energy. Without Masculine energy, you wouldn't be able to advance in your career, stay organized in your life, or get into any sort of regular established self-care or health routine.

Over my years of working with clients, I've found that some women have a hard time turning off their Masculine energy, while other women have a hard time turning their Masculine energy on. Wherever you are on your journey, I want you to know that it's totally possible to create a healthier relationship with this part of yourself. And when used correctly, your Masculine energy is actually essential in helping you to prioritize and connect with your Feminine energy.

As you gain a deeper understanding of the different elements of Masculine energy, you can then bring awareness to your own patterns and start to use this energy to your benefit. You can be more discerning about when to actively call upon your Masculine energy, and when you need to set it aside.

Feminine Energy

If the Masculine is described as "doing" mode, the Feminine can be described as "being" mode. When you're aligned with your Feminine energy, you'll feel more relaxed and "in flow" with life. In Hindu traditions, Feminine energy is referred to as Shakti or life force energy, and it's responsible for creation, nourishment, and a feeling of aliveness. It's a powerful cosmic energy that flows through every living, breathing being on the planet. You can think of the Feminine as a deep exhale that allows you to soften, relax, and tune in.

When you're connected to your Feminine energy, you have direct access to your Soul. Feminine energy is responsible for your intuition, your creativity, and your self-expression. The Feminine is receptive, open, and magnetic. It's the part of you that's nurturing, caring, and devoted to love. When you're connected to your Feminine energy, you're more in touch with your emotions and your cyclical nature. You'll likely feel a desire to spend more time in nature to connect with the earth (aka the Great Mother).

While the Masculine lives in your head, the Feminine lives in your body. Many of us have become so disconnected from our bodies that we live "from the neck up," constantly thinking and operating from our minds. After years of overthinking, overanalyzing, and making decisions from their logical minds, it's no wonder that many of the women I work with have a hard time switching out of their Masculine energy. For this reason, the fastest pathway to reawaken your Feminine energy is through bringing awareness to your body through mindful breathing and movement.

Many of my clients have described the experience of reconnecting with their bodies as a feeling of "coming home to themselves." As they notice their Feminine energy come back online, they feel instantly relieved and nourished. Through reconnecting with your body, you'll start to hear your inner voice (aka your intuition) more clearly; in doing so, you'll reclaim your power and remember your divinity.

While there are many beautiful aspects of being connected to your Feminine energy, it's important to know that it's possible to swing too far in this direction. When the Feminine is out of balance, you'll likely feel unproductive, stagnant, ungrounded, distracted, inconsistent, flighty, and/or reactive with your emotions. When left out of balance for too long, Feminine flow can lead to lethargy, frustration, depression, anxiety, and overwhelm. Thus, it's important to notice when you're slipping too far out of balance in this direction.

Energy Check-In

Before we begin our journey through the Feminine principles, let's get a baseline understanding of where you're currently at when it comes to your inner Masculine and Feminine energetics.

Here are a few questions to help you in your exploration:

- What percentage of the time throughout your day do you spend in your head?
- What percentage of the time throughout your day do you spend in your body?
- What percentage of the time throughout your week do you spend in "doing" mode?

- What percentage of the time throughout your week do you spend in "being" mode?

Typically, when I ask my clients these questions, they share that they're operating in their Masculine energy (aka thinking and doing mode) at least 80 percent of the time—which, by default, means they're only connecting with their Feminine energy 20 percent of the time. While there's no perfect equation for how often you're "supposed" to be in either of these energies, the more presence and awareness you have in relation to how you feel emotionally, physically, and energetically, the easier it will be to recognize if you're out of alignment with your own unique equilibrium.

Energetic Polarity

Up until this point, we've focused on the inner relationship between your Masculine and Feminine energies. As you become more practiced at creating harmony within yourself, you can start to explore the dynamics that Masculine and Feminine energies play in your romantic relationships. This is where the concept of Energetic Polarity comes in—the energetic dance between Masculine and Feminine energy as it relates to intimacy between two individuals. Polarity refers to the concept of having two opposing and complementary forces, like a magnet with a positive charge at one end and a negative charge at the other. In the arena of romantic relationships, having one partner in their Masculine energy and the other partner in their

Feminine energy helps to keep the passion, chemistry, and intimacy alive. This doesn't mean that women always have to be in their Feminine energy and men in their Masculine energy, but rather it's about being able to flow between these two energies based on what would create the most optimal "charge" within the relationship dynamic.

This concept and understanding of Energetic Polarity has been taught in tantric and yogic philosophies throughout history, although it's become more mainstream in recent years as couples are recognizing the impact that depolarization is having on their emotional and sexual intimacy. Perhaps this core issue has been at play for centuries, but as consciousness rises, people are becoming more curious about the imbalances at play as it relates to their relational struggles.

If we look back over the past few centuries, we can see how Energetic Polarity in relationships has shifted due to the evolution of gender roles in society. Historically, the role of men was to hunt and protect, while the role of women was to nourish and tend to the home. These traditional roles were further embedded in society through patriarchal ideologies. The Feminist movement allowed women to break free from traditional gender roles and regain more autonomy and sovereignty in their lives. However, the unintended result of this was to create an environment where nearly everyone is "overfunctioning" in their Masculine energy—taking on too much responsibility and trying to control everything. This has diminished the polarity in romantic relationships, as well as creating high rates of disconnection, dissatisfaction, and burnout. However, by understanding the concept of Energetic Polarity and putting it into practice, it's possible to reignite the spark between romantic partners without regressing to the proscribed gender roles of the 1950s.

Energetic Agility

Eventually, the goal is to be able to transition between these two energies on a moment-by-moment basis. One of my favorite terms for this technique is called "Energetic Agility," which means that you "are skilled in both Alpha (Masculine) and Omega (Feminine), and can pivot between the two embodiments at will, choosing whichever best serves the moment."[2]

For example, you might be in your Masculine energy at work—leading, focusing, and being productive—with little space for flow and emotion. When you come home from work or a busy day with your children, it can be easy to bring that Masculine energy with you into a relationship context, but it might not serve you to stay in your Masculine energy. Developing Energetic Agility looks like being able to pause before you cross the threshold, check in with yourself, and consciously choose to connect with your Feminine energy in order to relate with your spouse or partner on a heart level, rather than just with your head.

Alternatively, there are times where important tasks, commitments, and responsibilities can start falling through the cracks if you stay in your Feminine flow. This is a great opportunity to tap into your Masculine energy, get organized, and create an action plan so you can show up consistently and follow through with your goals.

Energetic Agility is about choosing to be emotionally open, receptive, and connected to your intuition so you can respond in the most aligned way from moment to moment.

Coming Back into Balance

When you begin your journey of learning how to consciously dance between your Masculine and Feminine energies, you can expect it to be a wobbly and imperfect experience. There will be times where you swing too far into your Feminine energy and feel frustrated with yourself for being unproductive or unorganized. Other times, you'll find that you push past your capacity with your Masculine energy and end up feeling burnt out and exhausted.

Every time you think you're "doing it wrong," I want you to remind yourself that this is all part of the process. As humans, we often learn through contrast; sometimes we have to touch the (metaphorical) red-hot stove before we finally learn that it will burn us. It's through the contrast of being out of balance that we learn how to come back into alignment.

The deeper you get into this practice, the more attuned you'll become to the subtle cues that your nervous system and your body are sharing with you. As your understanding of your inner polarity between your Masculine and Feminine energies becomes more nuanced, you'll be able to be change course before you reach either of the two extremes.

One example of how this Energetic Agility has changed my life is that I rarely get sick anymore. In the past, if I was starting to feel sick, I overrode or ignored my body's cues. I would go to the gym even though I was tired and continue pushing through until I actually got sick. This eventually led to me getting sick quite often, which made it hard for me to have any sort of consistent routine. Now, when I notice my energy is low or that my immune system is fighting something, I take a few days off from working out and give myself more rest. Before I know it, I'm back on track and feeling great.

This works the same way if you're starting to lean toward too much Feminine energy. Once you start to trust your inner Masculine, it'll help to prevent you from straying too far from your healthy routines. As soon as you start to sense that you're off track from your goals, you can easily access your inner discipline to get you back on track.

Embarking on The Feminine Way

The following chapters will begin to explore, one by one, the Seven Feminine Codes that will guide you to living in The Feminine Way. These codes will bring to light important information that has been nestled safely in your Soul for your whole life, just waiting to be witnessed, uncovered, and honored. By exploring these principles, you'll begin your journey toward infusing the Divine Feminine into all aspects of your life.

Ready? Let's do this, sister!

Soul Reflections

- What qualities of the Feminine do you want to cultivate more of in your life? (i.e., intuition, nurturing, receptivity, etc.)
- What qualities of the Masculine do you want more of in your life? (i.e., structure, organization, focus, etc.)
- Are there any specific areas of your life (i.e., career, romantic relationships, health etc.) where you find yourself more in your Feminine energy?
- Are there any specific areas of your life (i.e., career, romantic relationships, health etc.) where you find yourself more in your Masculine energy?

"You, too, can be carved anew by the details of your devotion."

Mary Oliver

chapter three

Deepening Devotion

I sat with my spiritual mentor, eyes closed, heart searching for answers. After almost eight years of struggling with chronic depression, I was ready to break this cycle and gain insight into how I could change the trajectory of my life.

In one of our first sessions together, my mentor guided me through a powerful visualization where she invited me to envision my life three years ahead. She said, "Picture what you want your life to look like. More importantly, focus on how you want to *feel* on a daily basis."

As I went deeper into this guided meditation, my body started to tingle all over and tears welled in my eyes. I realized that I'd never before stopped to think about what I wanted in my life. All my life, I'd been unconsciously following the path of what I thought was "right" and "good." I had unconsciously created a life that would make other people happy, instead of a life that was built around my own happiness. No wonder I was feeling so empty, exhausted, and depressed.

After this powerful guided visualization, however, I could see a different future for myself. I finally felt like I had a direction to move toward. And while connecting with my vision for the future was a powerful step toward my new reality, I knew that the journey of transforming my life wasn't going to be easy, and it certainly wasn't going to happen overnight. The gap between the woman I was and the woman I wanted to become had been illuminated. Now it was time to get to work.

I realized that if I really wanted to change my life, it was up to me to do the inner work. No one else could do it for me. I was finally ready to take full responsibility to do whatever was necessary to prioritize my own happiness and well-being. Rather than trying to "fix" myself or get to the finish line faster, I recognized that I needed to try something new.

This is the turning point where I started to see my healing journey through a Feminine lens. Instead of taking a rigid, Masculine approach to healing where I was doing the same morning routine every single day, I started to check in with my intuition to see what my body was asking for. Instead of going through my spiritual practices like I was checking things off my to-do list, I intentionally chose to be more present with each ritual that I was partaking in. Instead of getting upset if I noticed old perfectionist patterns coming up, I reminded myself that healing is a cyclical process, not a linear one. Instead of being hard on myself if I skipped a meditation, I gave myself grace and remembered that I could try again later or the next day.

No matter how tired or anxious I felt when I woke up, I chose to show up in devotion to my daily practices. As I deepened my devotion to spending time with my Soul every day, I got to know my authentic self on a more intimate level. It was through this process that my faith and intuition got stronger. Eventually, I stopped feeling resistance to my daily practices and started to look forward to them when I woke up. Day by day, it became easier for me to let go of the chatter of my mind and drop into a meditative state where I could connect with my Higher Self. It was through my daily devotion that I started to notice the micro-shifts in my emotions and my energy throughout the day.

As my inner landscape began to change, I observed how I was responding differently to people and situations that used to trigger feelings of unworthiness, overwhelm, and self-doubt. After a few months of connecting more intimately with my Soul, I developed the confidence to speak my truth in my relationships and to show up more boldly in my business. After a few years of showing up for my spiritual practices, I no longer identified as a woman who was depressed or insecure. Instead, I felt a deep sense of safety, self-trust, and confidence from within.

To this day—almost seven years later—I attribute my internal happiness and external success to my daily devotion of connecting with my Feminine energy and spending time with my Soul. The good news is that you don't have to wait until you hit rock bottom to start living in alignment with the woman you came here to be. Once you understand the foundational concept of deepening your devotion, your journey to creating a life that feels enjoyable, inspiring, and fulfilling will unfold more naturally and easefully.

In this chapter, you'll receive all the wisdom and insight you need to cultivate a Feminine devotional practice that deepens your alignment with your Soul.

Deepening Devotion

> ***Feminine Devotion:*** *the art of aligning one's thoughts, beliefs, and actions with love, truth, and beauty.*

Feminine Devotion is the foundational principle at the heart of your journey to living in The Feminine Way. As you shift out of the old paradigm and move away from your commitment to hustle, material success, and social status, it's essential to be clear about what you're devoting yourself to instead.

Anchoring in this principle of Feminine Devotion will support you in accessing and integrating all of the other Feminine principles and wisdom that this book has to offer. This Feminine Code is the one we'll come back to time and time again throughout our journey together.

Devotion is a way of being. It's a way of relating to the world from your heart, rather than from your mind. To live a life of Feminine Devotion takes practice and daily dedication.

Think of it like strengthening your muscles: if you want to get stronger, you can't just show up to the gym when you feel like it, you have to show up consistently. When you do, your body gets stronger. Similarly, deepening your devotion—which is, in essence, about deepening your connection with your body, your heart, and your Soul—takes time and patience.

One of the primary methods for cultivating a deeper devotion to the Feminine in your life is through implementing daily rituals and spiritual practices. In Western culture, we've long forgotten the art of ritual. In every ancient tradition, there are many different rituals that are performed on a daily, weekly, and monthly basis. When I traveled to Bali in 2016, I was amazed at the devotion Balinese people showed toward their daily offerings and prayer rituals. On many street corners, Balinese women would sit and weave together little baskets with banana leaves as a vessel to create offerings to God(dess). Each of these baskets were filled on a daily basis with flowers, sweets, and other sacred items as an offering of gratitude and respect to their Hindu gods.

Whichever spiritual path we choose to take, it's through our daily rituals that we learn to deepen our connection with ourselves on a Soul level and with the Universe at large. Later in this chapter, we'll discuss how to customize your own daily rituals. But before we get to that, let's explore the three key pillars that are at the core of Feminine Devotion.

Devotion to Love

What does it mean to be devoted to love? According to the metaphysical text, *A Course in Miracles,* our thoughts come from only two places: love or fear. As humans living in a fear-based society, our thoughts often default to fear. Fear-based thoughts are rooted in judgment, shame, worry, resentment, and pain, whereas love-based thoughts are rooted in gratitude, kindness, patience, trust, forgiveness, and compassion. It takes conscious effort to notice when the voice of fear is present and to choose more loving thoughts instead. When you have fear-based thoughts, you'll notice you feel guarded, contracted, and/or reactive. Conversely, when you choose love-based thoughts, you'll feel more connected, peaceful, and open.

For this reason, I consider it a devotional practice to actively choose to come back to love whenever you get triggered, whenever you feel afraid, and whenever you notice self-judgment. Whenever you notice that you're having fear-based thoughts, take a few deep breaths, put your hand on your heart and ask yourself, "What is a more loving and supportive thought I can have right now?" or "What would love do (or say) in this moment?"

Another interpretation of living in devotion to love is to let your heart lead the way instead of letting your mind take control. We've all heard the saying "Follow your heart," but because of fear-based conditioning, we've been taught that it's not "safe" or "responsible" to trust our emotions, our passions, and our desires. We'll dive deeper into this in the Awakening Intuition chapter; for now, just notice what choices you're making from your heart, and which you're making from your head.

Devotion to Truth

Throughout your life, it's likely that you've allowed other people's thoughts and opinions to affect your decisions. In some cases, these decisions may have been in alignment with what felt true for you, while in other cases you may have said yes even if they didn't align with your values, beliefs, and desires. Living a life of truth is about connecting to what you feel is right for you and being fiercely devoted to following your deepest alignment.

As you begin to shift your devotion toward your truth, it's common to worry that you'll upset or disappoint others. However, when you live in alignment with your truth, people will be able to trust you more. Living in devotion to truth also means speaking your truth instead of holding back your thoughts and opinions. When done from a place of love, it will allow for more authenticity, vulnerability, and intimacy in your relationships.

Devotion to Beauty

Living a life devoted to beauty is about honoring the beauty in nature and the natural beauty that exists within you. It's about intentionally creating an energy of peace through your home environment, the clothes you wear, and the way you take care of your possessions. By focusing on creating external beauty—not from a place of vanity, but from a place of devotion—you'll naturally foster a sense of calm and peace within you and for those around you. This doesn't mean that you need to spend a ton of money to redesign your home or upgrade your wardrobe all at once. Rather, it means being more intentional about the items you choose to purchase so that you reduce chaos in your surroundings and bring more tranquility and awe into your life.

Reconnecting with your Soul Essence

The Feminine is here to remind us of the sacredness of life and to reconnect us with our Soul essence. Even when we have gone astray and forgotten who we are and why we are here, the Feminine has a way of guiding us back to what truly matters. The more deeply we devote ourselves to honoring the Divine Feminine, the more we can connect with the divinity within ourselves. As we connect with our true divine nature, we come into alignment with our natural state of being, which is peace, ease, compassion, and love.

The disharmony, dysfunction, and dissatisfaction we experience in our own lives is a direct result of being removed from our own divinity. That said, no matter how disconnected you currently feel from your true nature, you always have a choice to come back home to your Soul and reconnect. *A Course in Miracles* teaches us that, in every single moment, we always have the choice to come back to love. So even if you feel like you've "messed up" or reverted to fear-based, hyper-Masculine ways of being, there is no reason to be hard on yourself; rather, you can see each instance of contrast as an opportunity to realign with love.

By deepening your devotion to the Divine Feminine, you're intentionally putting energy toward creating a life that feels good from the inside out, as opposed to creating a life that looks good from the outside. Unlocking the Code of Feminine Devotion will help to create a deeper sense of self-trust, confidence, and connection with your intuition. In time, your daily devotion practice will support you in letting go of control and trusting the Universe to support your highest good. As you continue on this journey, you'll find that you feel more comfortable speaking your truth, setting boundaries, and being your authentic self. And you'll attract like-minded people who have similar values and are living on the same vibrational frequency as you. This is the fun part, where you'll discover what it feels like to be "in flow" and notice that synchronicities are happening on a regular basis.

Devotion vs Discipline

It's probably not the first time you've heard that a daily spiritual practice would be beneficial for you. You've probably already tried meditation, yoga, and/or journaling, and noticed their positive effects, but perhaps you haven't been able to develop a consistent practice. If you're someone who struggles with consistency and committing to things that you know are good for you—like healthy eating, exercising, drinking enough water, or meditating—it's likely you've been approaching these practices from a place of Masculine discipline.

From a young age, most of us were raised with a disciplinary approach. We were taught that if we don't do something well, or if we make a mistake, there will be disappointment and/or punishment waiting on the other side. Similarly, as adults, we've been taught that we need to be super strict and disciplined if we want to achieve our goals, and if we don't show up perfectly then we'll fail or disappoint ourselves. And while this disciplinary approach might work well for those who are dominant in their Masculine energy, it certainly doesn't work for most Feminine beings.

The Feminine likes doing things that feel good. She likes to do things because she *desires* to do them, not because she is "supposed to" do them. If you're doing a practice because you feel like you "should" do it or you're "supposed to" do it, it's likely that your inner Feminine will feel rebellious and will find a way *not* to do it. Alternatively, imagine how different it would feel if you showed up to your devotional practices because you're deeply committed to feeling good and showing up as your Higher Self throughout the day. For example, you could clean your house or fold laundry from a place of resentment and frustration, or from a place of devotion to creating a home environment that feels beautiful, inspiring, and peaceful. Which feels more fun and approachable?

If hearing this distinction between discipline and devotion feels like a sweet exhale and a permission slip to stop forcing yourself to do things that don't feel good for you ... well, welcome to The Feminine Way!

In addition to the word "discipline," you may also have a negative association with the word "routine." For many people, having a routine is associated with being rigid, robotic, and mundane. Unlike routines, rituals are infused with sacredness, intention, beauty, and love. While routines can be approached mindlessly, with the intention of checking another line off your to-do list, rituals cannot. Imagine how different it would feel if you lit a candle, said a prayer, or took a few deep breaths before you jumped into your next task. This simple energetic shift can often help to get you out of autopilot and bring you into the present moment to enjoy your daily practices more.

Letting Go of Perfectionism

Showing up for your daily rituals is not about being perfect. Contrary to the disciplinary approach, in which you feel like you've done something "bad" or "wrong" when you skip a day or two of your practices, the devotional approach invites you to come from a place of curiosity and self-compassion. When you stop putting so much pressure on yourself to be perfect, and stop beating yourself up for falling out of alignment for a few days or even a few weeks, you'll find that it's much easier to come back to your daily rituals.

When coming from a place of curiosity, you might ask yourself: "I wonder why I didn't show up yesterday for my practices?" Perhaps it was because you didn't get enough sleep the night before. Perhaps it's because you feel bored and you need to switch things up a bit. Perhaps there was a voice of self-sabotage that made excuses because you're reaching a new level of growth, and growth can be frightening to certain parts of us. Once you get curious and ask non-judgmental questions, you can create a plan for when you next encounter the same challenge in the future.

Taking an approach of self-compassion may sound something like, "It's okay that I didn't show up for my rituals this morning. I can do them later today or try again tomorrow." This is a huge shift from the hyper-Masculine and self-critical voice inside your head that holds you to unrealistic standards.

The truth is, we're not supposed to be "perfect." As human beings, it's inevitable that we're going to mess up or fall off track sometimes. Rather than trying to be perfect all of the time, our success lies in how quickly we can forgive ourselves and get back on track with the actions that will bring us back into alignment.

Cultivating a Daily Devotional Practice

In many traditional religions and cultures there are specific guidelines and rules about how spiritual practices "should" be performed. For example, in the Jewish religion there's a specific set of prayers that are said every morning and every evening. In some yogic traditions, like Kundalini, Ashtanga, and Bikram, there are specific sets of stretches and postures that you're supposed to repeat in the same order every single day. While there's tremendous value in these proscribed methods, not everyone resonates with this level of rigidity. As you grow and evolve, the way that you choose to connect with your Higher Self will likely evolve as well.

Prior to learning about Feminine Devotion, you may have associated the word "devotion" with religious practice. However, in the context of The Feminine Way, a "devotional practice" is anything that helps you feel more connected to your Soul. Your devotional practice can look different to mine, and it can also change over time depending on what helps you to feel the most aligned and connected. It doesn't matter what you specifically "do" for your devotional practices; rather, it's about showing up and spending quality time with your Soul on a daily basis. As you do this, your connection with your Soul and your faith in the Universe will deepen.

Before we explore the various spiritual rituals that are available to you, it can be helpful to implement some basic Masculine structure to reduce overwhelm and to set you up for success. A great starting point is to get clear on how much time you would like to dedicate each day to your devotional practices. If you're new to creating consistent daily rituals, you can start with ten minutes each day and work your way up to twenty or thirty minutes. Depending on your lifestyle, you may wish to do an extended practice on the weekends or whenever you have more time.

It's also helpful to be consistent with the time of day that you do your rituals. There are powerful benefits to doing your rituals first thing in the morning—for example, fewer distractions from other people and obligations. Additionally, when you do your rituals first thing in the morning, you're intentionally aligning your energy and mindset to feel more positive, inspired, and energized for the day ahead. If you have children, you'll likely need to wake up earlier than them to get your morning rituals in; if they're old enough, you can include them in your rituals, or designate your ritual time after you drop them off at school.

In the following section, we'll review a variety of different spiritual tools that you may wish to explore during your daily rituals. As you review these options, remember that you do not need to do all of these practices every single day. Instead, use this list for inspiration, and choose only the practices you feel drawn to. Again, feeling connected to yourself is more important than the specific practices you choose.

Spiritual Rituals Menu

Meditation

Meditation is the foundation of my personal spiritual practice. The purpose of meditation is not to silence your thoughts, rather it's a tool to become an observer of your thoughts and to help you relate to your emotions without reactivity. One of my spiritual mentors described meditation as a daily practice of "taking out the mental trash," meaning that it's an opportunity to clear all of your unnecessary thoughts and mental attachments, and create space to connect more deeply with your Soul.

There are many styles of meditation you can try, including guided meditations, mantra-based meditations, Transcendental Meditation (TM), Mindfulness-Based Stress Reduction (MBSR) meditations, and walking meditations. If you're new to meditation, it can be helpful to start with guided meditations and/or take a meditation class so that you have a baseline for the practice. One of my favorite resources for guided meditations is Insight Timer, an app with thousands of guided meditations of varying lengths and topics.

When first starting your meditation practice, start with two to five minutes per day for a week and then work your way up to longer meditation practices. It takes time to train your brain to relax and to slow down the mental chatter, especially when you're used to your thoughts running a hundred miles per hour.

Gratitude Journaling

Research has shown that gratitude can help to reduce stress and improve both mental and physical health. While gratitude may seem like a simple practice, it can have a major positive impact on your life. When I was in the throes of my depression, it felt challenging to think about what I was grateful for because my mind was so focused on the negative.

But the more I practiced focusing on gratitude, the easier it became, and the happier I felt.

A simple way to practice gratitude is to write down three things you're grateful for every day. In order for this practice to work, it's important that you take a moment to connect with the *feeling* of gratitude, rather than just writing it down and moving on to your next task. It's helpful to be specific about what you're feeling grateful for; for example, instead of saying, "I'm grateful for my health," you might write, "I'm grateful that I have the energy to get out of bed and connect with my loved ones today." As you implement this practice into your mornings, you'll train your brain to look for things to be grateful for throughout your day, which naturally leads to having a more positive outlook on life.

Yoga or Gentle Stretching

Practicing yoga or gentle stretching is a beautiful way to get out of your mind and connect with your body. The primary focus of any yoga practice is to connect your breath with movement in a way that brings you into the present moment. There are dozens of different types of yoga that you can explore to see which style feels best for your body. On days when you have more energy, you may wish to do a more intensive Vinyasa or Hatha flow. When you're feeling less energized, a Yin or Restorative practice might feel better in your body. Once you become familiar with the various yoga postures and techniques, you can start creating your own daily yoga flow without needing to follow an instructor or a specific set of poses. The key is to listen to what feels good for your body and to create a movement practice that brings your awareness inwards.

Breathwork

Breathwork is another technique that can help to reduce the chatter of your mind and help you to connect more directly with your Soul. Because of the heightened levels of stress that we experience in our modern-day lives, we often unconsciously constrict our breath, which leads to more anxiety and feeling disconnected from ourselves. Using traditional yogic breathing techniques such as *kapalabhati* ("breath of fire") or *nadi shodhana* ("alternate nostril breathing") can help to regulate your nervous system and reduce your stress levels. Over the past few years, more intensive breathwork techniques like Wim Hof's breathwork, Holotropic Breathwork, or Three-Part Breath have become popular techniques for physical and emotional healing. But, like yoga, no specific breathwork practice works for everyone.

If you're not sure where to begin, devote a few minutes each day to intentionally slow down your breathing, calm your nervous system, and come back into your body. You'll be amazed at the results. You can also download a breathwork app such as Pause Breathwork to be guided through a more advanced practice.

Pulling Oracle or Tarot Cards

Both Oracle cards and Tarot cards can be used as guidance for a daily devotional practice to help deepen your spiritual connection.

For this practice, you can simply pull a single card at random from your favorite card deck, or focus on a specific question or life area where you desire to receive guidance while you shuffle the deck and pull one or multiple cards. Take time to look at the artwork and the written description that the card is offering you. Then, reflect on the message you receive and how it relates to your life.

If you're new to the practice of card pulling, there are thousands of different Oracle decks that you can choose from. Some of my favorite decks are from Rebecca Campbell and Alana Fairchild.

Scripting Your Future

Scripting is a powerful journaling technique that focuses on what you're manifesting in your life. While traditional journaling practices focus on writing about challenging thoughts and emotions, scripting helps us connect with how we want to feel and what we want to create.

When you practice this technique, you'll want to write about your dream life as if it's already happening. For example, if you want to have a healthy relationship, you might write, "I'm so happy and grateful that I'm in a loving and supportive partnership." Or if you want to start your own business, you might write, "It feels amazing to create my own schedule and feel passionate about the work I'm doing every day."

It can be helpful to focus on a specific future timeline of one year, three years, five years, or ten years down the road so that your mind can conceptualize a vision for what's possible for you in this timeline.

Let yourself have fun with this one. Get creative and dream big!

Affirmations

Similar to gratitude practices and scripting, positive affirmations are designed to help you focus your energy and attention on how you want to feel and what you want to create in your life. A daily affirmation practice can elevate your self-talk, calm your anxiety, deepen your self-love, and increase your confidence.

When working with affirmations, you'll want to make sure they're customized and specific to where you are on your healing journey. For example, at the beginning stages of your self-love journey, the affirmation "I love and accept all parts of myself" might not feel true. Instead, you could adjust this affirmation to something like, "I'm learning to love and accept all parts of myself." Or if you're working on setting healthy boundaries, you could create an affirmation like, "I'm learning to honor my needs and speak my truth."

When implementing a daily affirmation practice, start with five to ten key affirmations that you say each day, and then come up with new ones as you feel inspired. Once you've written down your affirmations, you can either read them out loud or say them to yourself while looking in the mirror. Similar to a gratitude practice, it's important that you focus on *feeling* the words when you're saying them rather than just reading them on autopilot mode.

Walking in Nature

Getting outside for a nature walk is just as beneficial for your mental and spiritual well-being as it is for your physical health. In our productivity-focused society, we tend to spend most of our time indoors in front of our computers and often forget to spend time outdoors. Spending a few minutes walking outside each day can be a game-changer for your nervous system and your connection to yourself on a Soul level.

A daily nature ritual could either look like walking around your neighborhood while paying attention to the flowers, the trees, and the sounds of nature, or it could look like finding a patch of grass, taking your shoes off, and standing barefoot on the earth while taking a few deep, slow breaths. As you move your body and breathe in the fresh air, you'll start to feel more relaxed, connected, and open-hearted. You may even notice that creative ideas or intuitive guidance come through as you take this space for yourself.

Non-Linear Feminine Movement

This movement practice is all about letting your body move in a way that feels good for you. This could look like dancing, shaking, stretching, or gently swaying to the music.

To begin, find a space where you feel comfortable expressing yourself without any interruptions. You can use a yoga mat, or simply stand anywhere in the room where you have space to move your body.

Next, turn on some music that matches your mood, and allow the music to guide your body in whichever ways your body naturally wants to move. If you notice that you're overthinking or worrying about looking silly, come back to your breath, and reconnect with the music and the sensations in your body. Start with one or two songs each day (about eight to ten minutes) and expand your practice from there.

Now that you have a clear list of daily rituals to choose from, it's time to cultivate a practice of checking in with yourself to see which rituals are going to best serve you on any given day.

Here's a simple practice you can implement when you wake up in the morning to get clear on which rituals will help you to feel most connected and aligned.

Daily Alignment Check-In

- Close your eyes.
- Put one hand on your heart and one hand on your lower belly.
- Take three deep, slow breaths in.
- Notice how your body is feeling, how your heart is feeling, and how your mind is feeling.
- Ask yourself, "What do I need this morning to feel connected and nourished?"
- Once you have an answer, open your eyes and get set up for whichever rituals you feel guided to.

Creating a Sacred Space

The Feminine inside of you loves beauty and simplicity. Having a designated space in your home for your daily rituals can be a supportive way to create more consistency and enjoyment with your practices. Creating a space that feels inviting and peaceful in your home will help you to drop into a relaxing state much faster than if you were sitting in a cluttered and messy space. You can think of it as creating a mini temple or sanctuary that you can retreat to amidst the everyday chaos.

Creating a sacred space could look like creating a beautiful altar in a corner of your bedroom or office, designating a whole room in your home as a healing oasis, or anything in between.

Here are some items you may wish to include in your sacred space:

- Crystals
- Non-toxic candles
- Incense
- Essential oils
- Palo Santo and/or sage
- Meditation pillow
- Soft blankets or a soft rug
- Salt lamps
- House plants
- Fresh cut flowers
- Photos of your ancestors
- Photos of you as a young child
- Sacred items you've collected

Something else to consider is having natural lighting or a way to adjust the lighting to set a relaxing vibe as you settle into your sacred space. You can always search for fun ideas on Pinterest or social media to get inspiration for how you want to design your space.

Paige's Healing Journey

When Paige first came to me for coaching, she was struggling with daily anxiety, heavy emotions, and constant overwhelm. Every day, she would wake up with her mind racing, worrying about all the things she needed to do and take care of, and putting pressure on herself to be perfect.

Even though she'd been seeing a therapist for a few years and had a journaling practice, she still found herself being overly reactive to the smallest triggers throughout her day, and was confused as to why she felt so out of control. More, she felt trapped in this anxious space and was unsure how to get out.

Before we dove into deeper emotional empowerment methods, we worked on creating a customized daily devotional ritual that helped her to become calmer and more present at the beginning of the day. We explored various practices like guided meditations, breathing exercises, gratitude journaling, and positive affirmations. Simply by taking time to slow down and connect with herself on a daily basis, Paige started noticing a shift in her anxiety and began looking forward to her daily rituals.

Within a few months of deepening her devotion, Paige cultivated a stronger connection with her Soul and her anxiety started to dissipate. It was at this point where she discovered that no matter what was happening in her life or where she was traveling, she had the power to create a sense of wholeness from within. Instead of going through her days from a place of survival and fear, she was able to be more present and connected with her loved ones, and is now living a life where she feels energized, passionate, and free. Her transformation all started with her daily devotion to showing up for her rituals and her willingness to try a Soul-led approach to address her mental health challenges.

Maintaining Your Devotion

When you start implementing your daily devotion rituals, you may notice that the voice in your head tries to get you to sabotage and make excuses. Just like when you're getting into a new workout routine (or returning to an old one), you might not feel like doing it every day, and your mind might feel resistant. However, your Higher Self knows that if you engage in practices that are supportive for you, you will feel better throughout the day and will reap the benefits in the long run.

If you notice resistance to showing up for your Feminine devotion rituals, no problem! When you hear that old voice trying to keep you in your comfort zone, put your hand on your heart, take a few deep breaths, and ask yourself: "What would my Higher Self choose in this moment?" Remind yourself that you have the power to modify your daily practices based on how you're feeling that day. If you don't feel like meditating that day, then don't! Turn on some music and move your body instead. Either way, don't *force* yourself to do anything. If it consistently feels challenging to do your ritual practices in the morning, see if a different time later in the day feels better for you.

If you're like many of my clients, you may notice that you have an "inner rebel" that resists doing anything she doesn't want to do. This is often the case for people who grew up with strict parents or in a rigid school environment. If your inner rebel likes to pop up when you try to implement your daily rituals, it can be helpful to have a conversation with her to take the pressure off. You may be surprised that, when you assure her that she doesn't "have" to do anything she doesn't want to do, her resistance starts to decrease and you feel more inspired to show up for your daily rituals.

If you're someone who struggles with black-or-white thinking or perfectionism, you may notice that skipping a day of your rituals leaves you wanting to throw in the towel and give up. Instead of letting your inner critic take over, I invite you to see this as an opportunity to practice self-compassion and bring in a sense of curiosity. Remember that it takes time to implement new habits, and that just because you skipped a day doesn't mean you failed. Every day is a new opportunity to start again.

The gentler you can be with yourself, and the more often you show up for your practices, the easier it will get. As you take this new approach, you'll begin to notice the subtle differences in how you feel throughout the day and how you respond to external circumstances. Eventually, you'll feel like something is missing if you skip a day of your sacred rituals, and you'll experience the contrast of how different it feels when you don't do your practices. This contrast is often the exact inspiration that we need to recommit to our daily rituals when we feel resistant.

As we've explored in this chapter, the Code of Deepening Devotion is the foundation for opening the doorway to bringing more Feminine energy into your life. By prioritizing sacred time every day to connect with your Soul, you'll learn how to shift out of "autopilot" mode and instead start to experience more peaceful and enjoyable moments throughout your day.

That said, Code #2 is simply the first step toward living in The Feminine Way and learning how to connect with your intuition, which will guide you to creating a life that's in alignment with your Soul.

Soul Reflections

- In your own words, what does it mean to live in devotion to the Divine Feminine?
- What do you feel will be different in your life when you deepen your devotion to love, truth, and beauty?
- What are the top three rituals that you feel drawn to experimenting with this week, and why?
- How much time will you allocate each day this week to your devotional practices?

"When your faith is greater than your fear,
anything is possible."

Amy Natalie Pamensky

chapter four

Awakening Intuition

The bed felt unfamiliar. The room was dark. For a moment I had no idea where I was. Then, I remembered: I was in Tulum, Mexico, and I was supposed to be on vacation.

With my heart pounding, I checked my phone. It was 3:00 a.m. I wanted to speak to someone—anyone—about how I was feeling, but there was no one I could call at this hour. There was nothing but the silence to fill the space, and no way to escape this intense, consuming anxiety.

This wasn't a new feeling. I'd been here many times before, except this time I had some tools I could lean on. So, I turned on a guided meditation to help me calm my whirling mind and get some clarity on why this feeling was coming on so strong. If I tried to resist the anxiety, I knew it would just get worse, so I followed my inhales and exhales with awareness and watched as the tension in my body started to soften.

As my thoughts settled, I asked the Universe for guidance. I whispered a prayer from *A Course in Miracles*: "Where would you have me go? What would you have me do? What would you have me say, and to whom?"

Within moments, a loud voice came through: "Sell all of your belongings and start traveling."

I took a deep breath. Tears ran down my face. I was completely taken off-guard by the guidance I'd just received.

Immediately, I grabbed my journal and started writing down my thoughts about these instructions.

While I wrote, I was thinking, "This is crazy! I've lived in San Diego for most of my life. I've never considered leaving, and now I'm supposed to become nomadic?!"

Even though the message didn't make logical sense, I knew I had to follow it. My whole life was about to change. I was being called to step out of my comfort zone and start a new chapter beyond anything I'd ever imagined.

If you imagined me being excited by this, you'd only be half right. While traveling full time did hold some appeal, it also felt terrifying to be entering into the unknown. A wave of grief and fear washed over me. For the next few days, I could barely sleep or eat anything at all. I let the sadness move through me whenever it rose to the surface. What was intended to be a fun tropical vacation had turned into a deep, heart-healing journey.

Yet underneath the pain of letting go, there was a deeper knowing that I was exactly where I was supposed to be.

When the vacation ended, I returned home with a sense of

confidence and purpose. Over the course of the next month, I broke up with my boyfriend of two years, sold my furniture, put the rest of my belongings in storage, and bought a one-way ticket back to Tulum. With no roadmap ahead of me, I knew I was being guided through my own "surrender experiment". I was being asked to let go of control and to deepen my faith in the greater plan that the Universe had in store for me. Every time my mind tried to come up with a plan or figure out where I was going next, I returned to prayer and asked for guidance. For the next eight months, I listened to the whispers of my Soul. I received invitations to travel to new places that I never anticipated exploring.

This level of trust in my intuition didn't happen overnight. Leading up to this experience, I'd been studying intuition and strengthening my trust muscle for over five years. At first, I practiced using my intuition with small, day-to-day decisions when it came to choosing what foods and exercise felt good for my body; and eventually, I started to make bolder decisions when it came to social situations, my business, and lifestyle choices.

Regardless of where you're at on your journey, you *can* learn how to trust your intuition to guide you rather than fear. In this chapter, we'll explore the various ways in which your intuition can speak to you, as well as simple practices to deepen your trust with your inner guidance system.

Intuition: Your Feminine Superpower

Put simply, intuition is the language of the Soul and the channel through which your inner guidance speaks to you. You can think of your intuition as an internal GPS system that's always guiding you toward a life that's in alignment with your greatest happiness, fulfillment, and abundance. Even if you feel disconnected from your intuition, I can assure you that it's not missing. Just like everyone else, you were born with access to your intuition and have your own natural intuitive gifts.

Intuition is often referred to as the "sixth sense" or "gut instinct" because it gives us the ability to know things without any tangible evidence. Unlike thoughts, which happen in the mind, intuition lives in the body and speaks to us through our emotions and physical sensations. It's for this reason that intuition is considered a Feminine quality, whereas logical thinking is considered a Masculine quality.

I think of intuition as a Feminine superpower. While the mind can offer knowledge, your intuitive body gives you access to *gnosis*, which is embodied wisdom from the spiritual and mystical realms. When you're tapped into your intuition, not only will it protect you from harm but it will also guide you to live the extraordinary life you were meant to live. Your intuition will always tell you if you're off track and redirect you back into alignment with your truth. While it often feels scary to follow your intuition (in large part because it usually doesn't make any logical sense), every time you choose to listen, you'll notice that things fall into place more beautifully than you could have possibly imagined. I've seen this time and time again: those who are courageous enough to follow their intuition are richly rewarded and supported by the Universe.

When you learn how to understand your intuition, you can start making decisions based on what feels true for you, rather than on what your Ego is guiding you to do. Cultivating a trusting relationship with your intuition will support you in making small day-to-day decisions—like what to eat and what social invitations to accept or decline—as well as bigger decisions around your career, relationships, and health. With each intuitive-led decision, you'll bring your life into deeper Soul alignment, which is the key to living a life of purpose, happiness, and freedom.

Why Are We So Disconnected from Our Intuition?

In an ideal world, the Feminine and Masculine would be in balance, and so too would logic and intuition. Both are vital to our well-being and our ability to consciously create the life we desire. Yet, because our society places more emphasis on the Masculine qualities of logic, practicality, and reason, we're discouraged from honoring our emotions and listening to our inner knowing.

From a young age, we're taught to make "smart" decisions that are safe, predictable, and approved of by our families, religion, and society. Often, these choices happen at the expense of what feels right and true for us as individuals. We tend to follow these rules because, on a subconscious level, we fear that we'll lose our safety, security, and even our lives if we go against the herd. Additionally, when we're told that only society's guidelines can help us create success and safety, we begin to distrust and doubt our intuition.

However, there's plenty of evidence that the traditional rules are not working for most of us. Even when we follow the expectations and requirements that are impressed upon us, eventually the noise of discontentment and depletion becomes too loud to ignore. While the strategy of ignoring our intuition and making decisions based on gaining safety and approval from loved ones may have worked for us as children, as adults it becomes detrimental, even harmful, to our happiness and well-being.

Even if you try to ignore your inner voice, your intuitive wisdom doesn't just go away. The longer you continue suppressing, ignoring, and diminishing your inner truth, the more disconnected you'll become from this Feminine superpower. If you find yourself in this position, I want to reassure you that your intuition is not lost or broken. With awareness and patience, there's a way to strengthen and awaken it again. Through the first Feminine Code of Deepening Devotion, we've already set the foundation for you to start reconnecting with your intuition by creating space for your daily rituals. Now it's time to learn and develop new skills to cultivate a deeper relationship with your inner guidance.

Understanding the Language of your Soul

While we all have access to inner guidance, there are nuanced ways in which we each connect with our intuition. Learning about the four primary intuitive languages—namely clairsentience, claircognizance, clairaudience, and clairvoyance—is a great way to get familiar with the unique ways in which your intuition speaks to you.

- *Clairsentience* (clear feeling) is the most common intuitive ability. It's often described as a "gut feeling" or a felt sense in your body that shows up in the form of a physical sensation or an emotion. With clairsentience, you can feel other people's energy or emotions even without them saying anything to you. Similarly, when you walk into a room, you can feel the energy of the space or the crowd. Often, clairsentience presents as goosebumps, chills, or a change in body temperature.
- *Claircognizance* (clear knowledge) is the ability to know something about a person or situation without having prior education or logical information. When this type of intuitive guidance comes through, you might ask yourself, "How did I know that?" or "Where did that insight come from?" The answer is that your Higher Self or your spirit guides are providing you with this information to guide and support you. Claircognizance can also present itself through creative ideas or inspiration that comes to you without trying.

- *Clairaudience* (clear sound) is the ability to hear messages or information from your Soul and the spiritual realms. Many people experience this as a voice inside their head that sounds different to their regular thinking minds. For example, I shared at the beginning of this chapter that I heard a clear voice telling me to sell everything and start traveling; this was clairaudience. You might hear a voice that says, "Don't take that job offer" or "Wait until next week to make a decision." You may also hear messages about, or for, other people which could be coming from their loved ones and ancestors who have passed.
- *Clairvoyance* (clear sight) is receiving visuals in your mind's eye that represent some sort of message or meaning. These visions can come in the form of mental images, colors, or symbols. In some cases, you may see other people's auras or even supernatural entities.

The more familiar you get with the ways in which your intuition speaks to you, the stronger your connection will become, and the easier it will be to interpret the messages that your Soul is sending you. In time, your intuitive abilities will strengthen, and you may even awaken new intuitive gifts that you didn't have access to before.

It's important to note that comparing your intuitive abilities with others' is not supportive for your spiritual growth and healing. Just because someone else has psychic abilities to see and hear messages doesn't mean that their gifts are more important or powerful than your ability to feel or "know" information. Your Soul has access to the perfect gifts that you need in order to guide you on your Soul journey. We all have different gifts to contribute to each other, which is part of the magic!

Feeling vs Thinking Decisions

When it comes to making intuitive decisions, remember that your intuition is felt through your body, not through your mind. Up until now, it's likely that most of your decisions have come from your thinking mind to help you determine if the decision is logical and safe. Since intuition speaks to you through feelings and emotions, you'll need to go beyond your rational mind to connect with how a decision "feels" in your body. Rather than asking, "Does this make sense?" you'll want to start asking, "How does this feel in my body?"

Light or Heavy Meditation

I've guided many clients through this powerful intuition meditation to support them with bigger decisions about which they feel unclear. This practice is designed to connect them with the sensations in their body as they consider each of the different options available in their decision-making process. To keep it simple, I guide them into a relaxed state in which they can connect with the felt sensations in their body. Then I ask them to connect with the options they have available to them and notice if the option feels "light or heavy?"

If the decision feels light, energizing, exciting, or expansive, it means their intuition is guiding them in that direction. If it feels heavy, it means the decision does not feel aligned and therefore it's not the best decision for them.

Here's a simple practice you can easily do for yourself any time you're faced with a challenging decision (or even a small, everyday decision):

- To begin, close your eyes, find a comfortable place where you won't be distracted, and take a few deep breaths to relax your body.
- Once you're feeling relaxed, feel into the first option (Option A) that you're contemplating, and ask, "Does this feel light or heavy?"
- Without overthinking it, notice the sensations in your body as you connect with Option A.
- Then, take a deep breath and bring Option B to your awareness. Repeat the same question, "Does this feel light or heavy?" and notice what sensations you feel in your body.
- When you're complete, open your eyes, take out your journal, and write down what you experienced.

If you prefer to have guidance for this intuition meditation, you can access an audio version of this practice at www.amynatalieco.com/bookresources.

Tori's Intuition Journey

My client Tori is a skilled nurse who had years of experience working in hospitals. When she came to me for support, she was feeling burnt out from the long hours and was interested in exploring her other creative outlets as a possible new career path.

During this time, the hospital she was working at offered her a full-time position and a promotion. If she didn't take the position, she would go back to working two days a week and on an as-needed basis when the hospital was short-staffed.

As she considered both options, she made a "pros and cons" list to try to gain clarity on which direction was right for her. Logically, it made sense for her to take the full-time position—this was something she'd been working toward for years, and she'd be making more money. Yet, every time she talked to me about the decision, I could tell how stressed out and overwhelmed she felt about taking on more hours.

During our next few sessions, I guided her through the "light or heavy" intuition practice, and it became clear to her that the only reason to say yes to the promotion was because of fear. She was afraid that if she didn't take the position, she wouldn't have enough money to pay for her current lifestyle. Not to mention that her Ego desired the new job title she'd been working so hard to achieve. But when she checked in with her body, her intuition told her not to take the position.

This is when I asked the question, "If you knew that you were fully supported by the Universe, what decision would you make?" Her answer became even more clear, and she decided not to take the promotion.

One week later, Tori sent me a message: "Amy, you won't believe what just happened. The hospital offered increased pay for part-time workers, and I'll be able to pick up at least one extra shift every week for the next six months. This means I'll be making almost as much money as I would have if I took the full-time position, but now I'm working less hours and will have time for self-care and to focus on my creative projects!"

Your intuition will never lead you wrong.

Strengthening your Intuition

Strengthening your intuition is a practice of deepening your relationship with your Soul. The more you spend time with your Soul and pay attention to your inner voice, the more you will understand what it wants, needs, and desires.

To take this relationship further, there are a few additional practices you can explore.

Ask Your Intuition Specific Questions for Guidance

One of the ways to open a dialogue with your intuition is by asking specific questions for guidance and support. If you're feeling stuck around a certain decision or unclear about the direction you want to go with your life, these are great opportunities to practice asking for guidance.

To start a conversation with your inner wisdom, you can either ask a question out loud before you start a meditation, before you pull an Oracle card, or write it down on a blank page in your journal.

Some questions you may wish to ask your intuition:

- What do I need to let go of to gain clarity?
- What is blocking me from seeing the answers?
- What is going to bring me the most peace?
- What will bring me the most joy?
- Which decision will serve my highest good?
- What are the next steps I can take on my healing journey?
- What can I do to call in more abundance?
- Who do I need to talk to today to give me insight about this decision?

Once you've asked your question, create space to listen for the answers. You can do this through meditating, doing breathwork, spending time in nature, or stream-of-consciousness journaling. I find that it's common for my intuition to speak to me when I'm in a "flow state" while I'm driving, dancing, or taking a shower. Sometimes the answers will come right away, and other times they may take several days. If you haven't received your answer, be patient and keep asking the same question for a few days. The more relaxed you can stay, the easier it will be to hear the answers. If you notice that you're overthinking instead of listening, bring your awareness back to your breath and come back into the present moment. Or take a break and trust that the answer will come through when you're ready to receive it.

Asking for Signs and Paying Attention to Synchronicities

Another fun way to interact with your intuition is to ask for specific signs to show if you're heading in the right direction. Some easy signs that you can ask for are animals, types of flowers, or angel numbers.

When I was going through my divorce, I asked the Universe to send me a butterfly to show me that I was making the right decision. In the next few days, I started seeing butterflies everywhere. When I was driving, a swarm of butterflies flew past my window. My therapist had a gift bag on her desk with a butterfly pattern on it. The Oracle card I pulled had a butterfly image on it. I also started seeing angel numbers everywhere I went: I'd see 111, 222, 333, and 444 on license plates, and would look at the clock at 11:11, 1:11, 2:22, 3:33, 4:44, and 5:55.

Pay attention to the synchronicities happening in your life. As you open your connection to your intuition, you'll notice that certain people and opportunities "randomly" pop up in your life exactly when you need them. When this happens, you'll know that your intuition is offering confirmation that you're headed in the right direction.

Alternatively, if you keep hitting roadblock after roadblock and you aren't getting any answers, this is a sign that you may want to pause and reevaluate your direction.

Practicing Your Intuition

Now that you know how to approach connecting with your intuition, it's time to start practicing!

In order to build trust in your inner knowing, it can be helpful to start with low-risk daily decisions instead of jumping into the deep end and trying to make big life decisions.

One helpful area to use your intuitive guidance is around daily food and exercise choices. Our current diet and exercise culture is full of hyper-Masculine rules about how, when, and what we should eat, and how and when we should move our bodies. The main focus has been on following systems to help us to lose weight—even though many of these guidelines disregard what is best suited for our unique body types and health conditions. Because we're so used to following the latest fad diets and routines, many women, including myself, have learned how to disregard the cues of their bodies and therefore have a hard time hearing what their body is asking for. For example, maybe you were told that you need to do intense cardio exercise to boost your metabolism, or that you should be eating a super-low-carbohydrate diet. And perhaps that worked for a while, but now you're noticing that your energy is depleted and you're having more intense food cravings. In this case, it'll be helpful to learn to pay attention to the intuitive signs your body is giving you so that you can figure out what actually works best.

One simple practice you can do to check in with your body is to close your eyes, put one hand on your heart and the other on your lower belly, take a few breaths, and ask yourself, "What does my body need right now?" You'll discover that some days you have the energy to go for a run, while other days your body desires more gentle exercise like pilates or yoga. Similarly, on some days your body may desire more hearty and warm meals, while on other days it wants to eat lighter and colder foods. Something else you'll discover is that during different phases of your menstrual cycle and different seasons throughout the year, your body will crave different types of movement and nutrition. We'll be talking more about this in later chapters as we explore the Feminine Code of Cyclical Living.

Another place that you can practice making intuitive-based decisions is with your social life. When someone asks if you'd like to attend an event or meet up for coffee, pause and check in to see if you really feel like going. Ask yourself, "Is this decision in my highest alignment? Do I have the energy for this? Do I actually *want* to go?" As women, because of our programming around people pleasing and always putting other people first, we often find ourselves saying yes to things that don't feel right or that drain our energy. If you slow down and check in with yourself before agreeing to social arrangements or saying yes to doing favors for other people, you might discover that you actually feel tired, overwhelmed, or stressed, and that it would feel better for you to get some rest or read a book instead.

I totally get that saying "no" might feel difficult and uncomfortable at first, but the more you start to honor your intuition, the better you will feel, and the more you can show up for your loved ones to give from a full cup.

Differentiating Between Fear and Intuition

One of the most common questions I get from women is, "How can I tell if it's my intuition or my fear speaking to me?"

A good way to differentiate between your intuition and fear is to understand the roles that your Soul and your Ego play in your life. In the simplest terms, your Ego is focused on safety and familiarity, while your Soul is always guiding you to expansion and growth. Additionally, your Ego speaks to you through your thinking mind, while your Soul speaks to you through sensations and emotions in your body. If you find that you're overthinking things, trying to control the outcome, or worrying about what could go wrong, this is your Ego doing its job of keeping you in your comfort zone. Alternatively, if you feel a spark of inspiration, are excited to try something new, or feel a sense of relief, this is your Soul speaking to you.

The tricky part is that, when you're living out of alignment with your truth or you're about to make a decision that's not right for you, your Soul will speak to you through anxiety or through a gut feeling that something is off. This anxiety can often resemble the feeling of fear, however these two emotions are not the same. Because the distinction between these two emotions is so nuanced, it's important that you don't rush into any decisions you don't feel clear about. If you aren't sure whether fear or intuition is speaking to you, return to your devotional practices to calm your mind and to come back to your body. If you keep checking in with your body, you'll eventually be able to feel what the right decision is for you.

Another place where you may experience confusion between your fear and your intuition is when your Soul guides you to make a big change and step out of your comfort zone. It doesn't want you to play small or stay stagnant. However, even if your intuitive knowing initially feels exciting and expansive, your Ego will quickly pop into the picture and present a variety of fear-based thoughts about why your idea isn't going to work out and why it would be safer to not go for it. If this happens, return to your breath once again, drop into a meditation, and come back into your body to reconnect with the initial feeling you got when you received the intuitive guidance. Just because fear is coming up doesn't mean that the decision isn't right for you. It just means that you need to continue strengthening your faith and developing your confidence to step outside of your comfort zone.

While the above framework is helpful in bringing more intellectual understanding, the best way to learn to tell the difference between your intuition and your fear is through real-life practice. We've all had times where we had a gut feeling that something was off but moved forward with the decision anyway—whether it was starting a new relationship, taking a job offer, or moving to a place we weren't fully excited about. Eventually, we recognize that the choice was not in alignment and that we should have listened to our intuition in the first place. Conversely, there may have been times when listening to your intuition felt crazy, but afterward you received clear evidence that you made the right decision. The truth is that you really can't mess it up! Even if you ignore your intuition and take a detour along your path, you'll eventually figure things out, and you can use that experience as a learning opportunity the next time you're faced with a similar situation.

Follow the Nudges

As you start opening to the guidance of your intuition, you'll receive little nudges or hints that will help you gain clarity. You don't need to see the full picture of exactly how things are going to work out in order to take action. As Steve Jobs said, "You can't connect the dots looking forward; you can only connect them looking backward. So, you have to trust that the dots will somehow connect in your future. You have to trust in something—your gut, destiny, life, karma, whatever." If you focus on following the intuitive nudges and taking small actions as they present themselves, the pathway will continue to unfold for you, and all will become clear in hindsight.

For example, your intuition might guide you to read a specific book, go to a yoga class, or call a friend you haven't talked to in a long time. When you follow these nudges, they will lead you to exactly where you're supposed to be so you can discover the clues for the next steps. As you can tell, following your intuition takes a lot of faith and trust. This is why it's so important to keep coming back to your daily devotion rituals to deepen your connection with your Soul and with the Universe.

When I was going through my divorce, I moved back in with my parents and was living in a different area of San Diego. This meant I could no longer go to the workout studio I loved so much. So, I started looking up local studios and got the nudge to try a Barre class nearby. When I walked into the studio, I was greeted by a friendly and wonderful instructor who asked if I'd like to put on an essential oil before starting class. I'd only recently learned about the healing benefits of essential oils, so in my mind I was like, "Wait, where am I right now? I've never had anyone ask this at any other studio I've been to. This is so wild!" The class was fun and energizing, and I felt so connected to my body. After the class, I stayed to chat for a bit, and the teacher asked if I wanted to meet for coffee. Over the next few months, she became one of my closest friends and introduced me to many other wonderful women. Keep in mind that this was a time of huge transition for me. I was afraid of what my life would look like after I went through with my divorce, and I was terrified that I wouldn't be able to make new friends. The Universe had a different plan for me. Over the next few months, as I continued to follow the nudges, I met so many incredible new women, and before I knew it, I had a whole community of girlfriends—something that I'd always deeply desired but didn't know was possible.

Using Intuition to Take the Leap

Whenever you're faced with a big change in your life, it's going to feel scary. Your mind will want to know the exact steps of how it's all going to unfold, but I'm sorry to break it to you: that's not how it works. An extraordinary life requires you to have faith and to take risks. (Just ask any successful entrepreneur or leader!) When you're willing to take a big leap, you'll discover that the Universe is waiting to catch you. As soon as you say "Yes" to living in alignment with your truth and following your intuition, new doors will open. You just have to take the first step.

This process isn't about abandoning logic. It doesn't mean turning off all your analytical, logical methods or avoiding paying attention to the factors at play. It simply means giving yourself the ability to tune in to your intuition to check whether or not a decision is in alignment with your Soul, and to allow yourself to go beyond the status quo of what seems reasonable or possible. There's no way to use logic to make a Soul decision. Intuition is the compass that helps you to know what's right for you.

Lauren's Awakening Journey

My client Lauren had been wanting to leave her corporate job for years before we started working together. She knew deep down that she was here to make a big impact in the world and she didn't want to work for someone else anymore, but she was too afraid to leave the comfort of her corporate job. For eight years, she'd worked for a marketing agency where she made really great money and had amazing benefits. She was terrified that, if she left her corporate job, she wouldn't be able to support her lifestyle.

Her intuition kept speaking to her, so she started to do some consulting work on the side to test the waters and see what it might be like to start her own company. Eventually, she got to a point where it felt impossible to keep working her corporate job if she wanted to go all in on her new business. Even though she didn't have evidence that she would be able to fully support herself through her consulting work, she took the leap and gave her notice. Within the first year of running her consulting business, she ended up working significantly fewer hours and making more money than she made in her corporate job. This gave her the time and energy to be able to focus on her true passion, which was starting her own podcast and creating events to support women on their abundance journeys.

Before you take any leap, it can be helpful to make some plans ahead of time to set yourself up for success—but remember that you'll *never* fully be ready for a big leap into the unknown. Whenever the fear comes up, your task is to recognize that your Ego is doing its job to try to keep you safe. Take some deep breaths, come back to your meditation practice, and reconnect with what feels true for you.

As we've explored in this chapter, awakening your intuition is the key to creating a life that's in alignment with your Soul, which in turn means creating a life of truth, love, and freedom! Making intuitive decisions may be new for you now, but before you know it, this way of living will become second nature.

The next Feminine Code, Emotional Alchemy, is designed to help you ride the waves of your emotions with more confidence and ease, so that you can continue to lean into your faith in the Universe and follow where your intuition leads you.

Soul Reflections

- What is the primary way your intuition speaks to you?
- Where are you currently feeling stuck or unclear in your life?
- What question would you like to ask your Higher Self for guidance during this time?
- If you didn't feel afraid, what decision would you make?
- Is there a deeper truth you've been avoiding out of fear that you might have to make changes?

"Life is alchemy, and emotions are the fire that turns me to gold. I will continue to become only if I resist extinguishing myself a million times a day. If I can sit in the fire of my own feelings, I will keep becoming [the woman I am meant to be]."

Glennon Doyle

chapter five

Emotional Alchemy

Sitting in an empty parking lot, watching the raindrops landing on my windshield, I felt warm, salty tears run down my cheeks.

It had been one week since I let my husband know I wanted a divorce. The grief. The sadness. The guilt. All of it came rushing to the surface. Before I knew it, the soft, silent tears turned into loud, uncontrollable sobbing. The sounds that came out of my body felt unfamiliar and foreign. I heard the voice of my Higher Self saying, "Deep breaths, honey. You've got this. Everything is going to be okay."

Lifting my gaze to the rearview mirror, I caught a glimpse of my water-filled eyes and smudged mascara. As I looked at myself, I realized this was the first time in my adult life I'd let myself cry in this way. These tears represented the grief, sadness, and guilt that had been wanting to rise to the surface for years.

In the next moment, the strangest feeling came over me. Somehow, in the midst of experiencing an intense wave of uncomfortable emotions, I simultaneously felt a deep sense of peace. Intuitively, I placed one hand on my heart, took a deep breath, and felt a smile come to my face. By allowing myself to fully feel my emotions without holding back or stuffing them down, I felt liberated, empowered, and relieved.

Turning Pain into Beauty

We all come into this world as feeling-based beings. From the time you were born, you had access to your emotions as a way to communicate your survival needs to your parents. As a child, you cried when you were hungry, you screamed when you were upset, and you used your emotions to express when you wanted someone to hold you. As you got older, you were likely taught by your parents, teachers, and society that it wasn't okay to fully express your emotions—that in order to be a "good" little person, you needed to behave yourself and keep your emotions under control. If your parents didn't have the capacity or skill set to hold space for your emotions (and regulate their own emotional landscape), it's likely that your emotions were not validated, acknowledged, or encouraged.

Even if you grew up in a supportive and loving home environment, your parents may not have been equipped to help you understand your emotions. Instead of allowing you to feel your emotions, they may have coddled you, scolded you, or tried to "fix" how you were feeling instead of simply allowing you to feel whatever was arising. If your emotions were neglected, criticized, or chastised, you may have learned that it wasn't safe to feel your emotions, and that expressing your emotions could cost you the love and connection you needed for survival. Additionally, if you grew up in a home environment where a family member had unstable emotions, you learned from observation that big emotions are dangerous, out of control, and unsafe. If you can relate to feeling this way as a child, it's not surprising that you feel cut off from the Feminine wisdom that your emotions have to offer, and that you instead learned to operate in the wounded Masculine energy of suppressing and neglecting your emotions.

As a little girl, I was really sensitive. I remember having lots of big emotions and feeling like I was "too much." Whenever I would cry, my parents did their best to soothe me to get me to stop crying. They were trying to be supportive and caring, but when they said, "You don't need to cry," I took it as a sign that getting upset was wrong. Whenever I expressed more intense emotions such as anger or frustration, I was sent to my room until I could "calm down." Even though my parents had good intentions, the message I internalized was that my emotions were too much, and that if I expressed any emotions other than happiness or staying calm, I was at risk of getting in trouble. This led to years of suppressed emotions that eventually came out in my teenage years as angst, frustration, and rebellion. Like many people, I walked around feeling "emotionally constipated" and unsure of how to process or express my emotions in a healthy way. By the time I was a senior in high school, I was diagnosed with clinical depression and adjustment anxiety disorder and was prescribed several medications to help me cope with my emotions.

It wasn't until my late twenties, when I discovered the healing practice of Emotional Alchemy, that I finally learned how to heal and feel empowered in my emotions. The process of Emotional Alchemy is a spiritual concept that entails turning your pain into beauty, transmuting your darker emotions into lighter emotions, and learning how to ride the waves in between. Emotional Alchemy doesn't promise that you'll never experience heavy emotions again; rather, it equips you to navigate any challenges with more grace for yourself and your emotional landscape. Inevitably, we will all experience some form of emotional pain in our lives, but with the right tools and practices, we can move through these challenges more effectively, and recover much faster.

In this chapter, I'll be offering insight and perspectives so that you can redefine your relationship with your emotions, reclaim your power, and reconnect with the Feminine wisdom they offer.

Reframing the Narrative

Up until now, our educational systems have focused primarily on developing Masculine cognitive skill sets and placed very little emphasis on Feminine elements such as emotional intelligence, intuition, or nourishing our bodies. Children learn about history, science, and math, all of which are focused on developing linear, analytical, and logical thinking skills. While these subjects and skills are important, when not paired with education around empathy, effective emotional processing, and healthy conflict resolution, it contributes to difficulties in navigating inevitable life challenges as they arise.

In addition to downplaying and neglecting emotional intelligence in our education system, children receive societal messages at a young age that it's not safe to express their emotions. Some of these messages include little girls being told that they are "too sensitive" or "too dramatic," and little boys being told that "emotions are weak" and that "real men don't cry." Unfortunately, the messages we receive in our crucial developmental years stay with us for our entire lives, unless we learn a new way of relating to our emotions.

This internalized conditioning—that powerful emotions are dangerous and unsafe— means that most of us try to avoid showing our emotions at all costs. We learn quickly to push down our "bad" or "ugly" feelings in order to be accepted, loved, and safe. How many times has someone asked you, "How are you doing?" and instead of sharing how you really felt, you offered a surface-level response of "I'm good!" so they couldn't tell there was something wrong? Or how about the times when you've been triggered at work or in a conversation with a friend, and instead of letting the tears or anger arise, you stuff them down and walk away feeling disappointed in yourself? This whole game of putting on a happy face for the outside world has led to us being disconnected, not just from our feelings but from our true, authentic selves.

Interestingly enough, we receive similar messages in the personal development and spiritual world. Through the Law of Attraction manifestation teachings, we learn that the goal is to be "high-vibe" all the time, which often leads to bypassing emotions that want to be felt. While methods like positive affirmations, NLP (neuro-linguistic programming), and reframing your thoughts are powerful tools to support your mindset, it can be easy to use these modalities to avoid your feelings and skip over the deeper work. This leads to a culture of toxic positivity, masking, and pretending things are fine when, spiritually, you're in distress. Your deeper feelings are still there, unacknowledged and unseen, because despite all your mindset work, you still don't feel safe enough to let them out.

While it might be possible to sweep your emotions under the rug for a time, unprocessed emotions do not disappear. They get stored in the body. In his book, *The Emotion Code,* Bradley Nelson explains: "Each time you trap an emotion, you get stuck in the middle of whatever traumatic event you were experiencing. So instead of moving beyond your angry moment, or a temporary bout with grief or depression, you retain this negative emotional energy within your body, potentially causing significant physical and emotional stress."[3]

Embracing Your Emotions

As human beings we have the capacity to deeply feel all of our emotions. However, this process of connecting with our emotions requires us to be able to access and trust our Feminine energy. Each of our emotions is here for a reason: to teach us something. There is absolutely nothing wrong with having big emotions; after all, you're a spiritual being having a human experience, and life gets hard sometimes. By embracing and welcoming your emotions instead of resisting or shaming them, you'll create a safer environment to let your emotions flow and be released.

Honoring your Feminine nature is about celebrating the full spectrum of emotions. It's an illusion to think that we should be happy all the time, and detrimental to think that emotions such as anger, grief, shame, and sadness are "bad" emotions. When we can honor our heavier emotions, just as much as we honor our lighter emotions, we create space for deeper healing and self-acceptance. The truth is that your heavier emotions want to be acknowledged; they want to be seen, and they want to be felt. When you judge your darker emotions, it adds a layer of shame, which perpetuates the toxic Masculine idea that emotions are bad, wrong, and untrustworthy, and causes you to push them away even more strongly. While these feelings may be uncomfortable or unpleasant in your body when they arise, it doesn't mean there's something inherently wrong with experiencing these feelings.

By acknowledging that it's perfectly normal for you to have deep emotions such as sadness, anger, or anxiety, we can start to strip away any self-judgment and shame you've been carrying around, and instead invite in compassion and curiosity. Through the Emotional Alchemy process, you'll learn how to identify, understand, process, and release your feelings. Instead of feeling like a victim to your emotions, you'll come out the other side feeling empowered with new Feminine insights and wisdom that allow you to show up more compassionately and confidently in your life and relationships.

Scout's Emotional Alchemy Journey

Scout was diagnosed with bipolar disorder in her early twenties. She was always afraid of her emotions because the fluctuations were so intense. The state of her mental health was making it challenging for her to function in society. It was impossible for her to keep a job, and she had to rely on other people to help her get through the day. Eventually, her family and her boyfriend also became afraid of her unpredictable emotions, which led to her further internalizing the story that her emotions were dangerous and out of control.

After years of therapy and medication, Scout made progress in being able to show up more consistently in the world, and eventually started her own business. It was during this time that our paths crossed. On our first call, Scout shared some details of her mental health journey; I could see how much fear, judgment, and shame she was carrying around her emotions. When she was done speaking, I looked her in the eye and said, "I know you've been afraid of your emotions for a long time, but I want to reassure you that there's nothing wrong with you. Emotions are a regular part of the human experience. You just need to learn how to understand them and relate to them differently." As I spoke, I could see her energy completely shift. She shared that this was the first time on her mental health journey where someone else was not afraid of her emotions.

Over the next six months, Scout learned how to listen to her emotions and how to process them in a healthy way. She deepened her connection with the Universe and continued to remind herself that it was safe to feel her emotions. As she invited in more compassion and love toward her emotions, her fear started to dissipate, and she grew more confident in her ability to ride the waves when her emotions arose. In time, not only did she become more empowered in her emotions but she also taught her loved ones that they no longer needed to be afraid of her emotions anymore. Through her devotion to her healing journey, Scout now has thriving relationships, a successful business, and feels capable of navigating whatever life brings her way.

Acknowledging Your Emotions

If you've been avoiding or ignoring your emotions, it's completely normal to feel numb, disconnected, or dissociated. The first step to reconnecting with your emotions is to identify and acknowledge your emotions when they're present. You can do this by taking a brief pause at various points in your day and doing a simple emotional check-in to become more aware of how you're feeling.

If you're navigating emotional or physical trauma, or if for any reason you don't feel safe approaching your emotions, I recommend finding a qualified mental health professional to do this work alongside you.

Below you'll find a step-by-step process for doing an emotional check-in. You can also find an audio version of this practice at www.amynatalieco.com/bookresources.

Emotional Check-In

1. Find a quiet place where you won't be distracted. Close your eyes and place one hand on your heart.
2. Take a few deep breaths and ask yourself, "How am I feeling in this moment?" or "How is my heart feeling?"
3. Notice if there are any sensations in your body (like tightness, tension, heat, or other physical discomfort).
4. As you explore the sensations in your body, see if you can identify a specific emotion that you're feeling. For example, is it sadness, frustration, anxiety, anger, or grief? (If you find it hard to identify your emotions, there are a number of helpful online

tools like the Wheel of Emotions by Psychologist Robert Plutchik to help you get clear on what you're experiencing.)[4]

5. Once you've identified the emotion, take a few deep, slow breaths and send your breath to the area of your body where you feel the sensation most strongly.
6. Take a moment to honor your emotions without judging them or making up a story about something being wrong. Bring compassion and gentleness to how you're feeling.
7. When you feel ready, open your eyes, and write down in your journal what you noticed during this check-in.

If you're new to this exploration of being present with your emotions, be patient with yourself and keep checking in multiple times per day. When you start doing emotional check-ins, two things may happen. Either you'll notice that it feels challenging to identify your emotions because you feel numb or disconnected from them, or your emotions will feel amplified because you're paying attention to them. In either of these situations, remember to be gentle with yourself. Give yourself the space to feel whatever is present for you. If you've been suppressing your emotions for a long time, they're likely screaming for you to pay attention and it might feel overwhelming at first because there's so much emotional backlog. Sometimes, it might even feel like you're going backward in your healing progress (especially if you've been taught that successfully managing your emotions looks like being happy all the time). Even if it doesn't feel like it right now, I can assure you that allowing yourself to feel your emotions is the key to moving forward on your healing journey.

The Wisdom of Your Emotions

As you continue to spend more time with your emotions, you'll find it easier to identify which emotion is present and to get more familiar with what is contributing to them in the first place. Your emotions are a fantastic source of Feminine wisdom, and the more you open up to listening to them, the more you'll begin to hear what they've been trying to tell you all along.

You can think of your heavier emotions as teachers that are here to show you when you're out of alignment with your authentic state. If you're not feeling good, there's likely a reason—either a situation, relationship, or choice in your life that's asking to be shifted. So, after you've done your emotional check-in, the next step is to get curious about what might be contributing to the uncomfortable emotions you're feeling.

The following are some questions you can ask yourself to bring more curiosity to your experience:

- How is my self-care at the moment? Have I been getting enough sleep? Eating enough food? Moving my body? Getting outside in nature?

- Have I been working too much and not doing enough activities I enjoy?
- Have I been isolating myself and not spending enough time connecting with friends and family?
- Am I avoiding making a decision or having a challenging conversation?
- Is there anywhere I haven't been setting healthy boundaries?
- Is there something I wish would change in my life but haven't yet taken responsibility for changing?
- Am I making my happiness and safety someone else's responsibility instead of taking steps to create them myself?

Again, emotions are messengers from your Soul. While it might seem like heavier emotions are here to make your life more challenging, if you're willing to get curious and sit with them, you'll find that they have valuable and insightful wisdom to share.

- Anger can reveal where you have not been speaking your truth, and can invite you to set clear boundaries with your time and energy.
- Anxiety can reveal where your mind is trying to control the outcome, and can invite you into a deeper place of trust and faith.

- Depression can reveal where you've been judging yourself, and can invite you into a more loving and compassionate relationship with yourself.
- Frustration can reveal where you've been waiting for someone or something outside of yourself to change, and can invite you into a greater level of personal responsibility for your own well-being.
- Shame can reveal where you feel a sense of unworthiness or where you've fed into the belief that you need to be perfect in order to be loveable.

As you begin to see your emotions as valuable messengers, they will guide you to make aligned decisions and support you in creating an authentic, Soul-led life.

Inner Child Healing

Within every powerful woman lives a little girl who's seeking love, safety, and attention. Even though we're living in adult bodies, our emotions are linked to experiences from our childhoods.

As children, we learn about love through our relationships with our parents, caregivers, and the world around us before our conscious mind is fully formed. From the ages of zero to seven, any emotional pain or trauma we experience gets stored as subconscious beliefs in our body, no matter how much our parents love us. As a result, when we get triggered by others, our nervous system responds through our innate protective mechanisms: fight, flight, freeze, or fawn. This often results in being overly reactive toward the emotional triggers we experience as adults, because we're actually responding from the level of emotional maturity as our younger selves.

This sympathetic nervous system response is a cry from your inner child for love, safety, and attention. Through inner child healing, there's the opportunity to go back in time to a moment when you felt hurt, scared, sad, angry or neglected, and provide that version of yourself the love she didn't receive in that moment. Some ways to connect with your inner child are through inner child meditations/visualizations, writing a letter to your younger self, and/or looking at a photo of yourself from when you were younger and speaking out loud to her. This practice of bringing compassion, love, and presence to your inner child is also known as reparenting. The next time you feel an emotional trigger arise, I invite you to sit with your inner child before you respond externally to the person or situation that you feel triggered by.

Some questions you can ask your inner child:

- "How can I best love you right now?"
- "What do you need at this moment?"
- "Is there anything you need to hear to feel loved/seen/heard/safe/accepted?"

Some reminders you can offer to your inner child:

- "I'm here."
- "I'm listening."
- "I love you."
- "You're loveable exactly as you are."
- "It's not your fault."
- "You're safe in this moment."
- "I'm never leaving you."

You can also find a guided inner child meditation by going to www.amynatalieco.com/bookresources.

After re-establishing your relationship with your inner child, it becomes much easier to call upon the voice of your inner nurturer/inner mother in moments when you feel triggered or upset. By opening yourself up to these heavier emotions, naming them, and acknowledging them without judgment, you begin to transmute them into the gold of self-acceptance, self-love, and self-care. Slowly, with care and attention, you can take each and every distressing, uncomfortable emotion and let it fill you with the Feminine power that's been waiting inside all of your life.

The Feminine is embedded in our whole emotional landscape. It's beautiful, raw, authentic, and vulnerable. When we can learn to connect into that vulnerability, it creates more intimacy and depth in all of our relationships. We become more sensitive and in tune with our emotions, and therefore more connected with our inner power. Instead of trying to show up in a strong, stoic, Masculine way in order to be successful or gain approval, we can find a deeper power within ourselves. We become not mountains but oceans, with all the power of the depths at our disposal. When we're connected to our body, our emotions, our intuition, we bring online a key aspect of our purpose here on this planet. This is the Feminine power—beyond the thinking, logical mind—that the world so desperately needs.

You Have to Feel It to Heal It

On a physiological level, emotions are simply "energy in motion." When you block the flow of your emotions by suppressing, numbing out, or avoiding them, the energy gets stuck in your body. This actually makes the emotions last longer, and over time can contribute to chronic physical or emotional health symptoms. However, when you give yourself permission to feel your emotions, you allow the energy to move through you, which means it can be released from your body faster. It's the difference between letting the big waves push you underwater and learning to surf.

As you've seen in this chapter, your Ego and conditioning have done an excellent job at helping you to avoid the pain of big emotions. If you've been hiding, deflecting, or otherwise sidestepping your feelings, you may have developed creative strategies that numb, distract, or distance you from your body and the emotions it contains.

These strategies may include:

- Drinking alcohol or abusing substances
- Overeating or eating when you're not hungry
- Using sugar or comfort foods to distract you from your feelings
- Drinking too much caffeine
- Immersing yourself in work
- Sleeping too much
- Numbing out with TV
- Scrolling on social media or watching YouTube videos
- Shopping (in person or online)
- Staying overly busy

While these strategies provide relief in the short term, they can slow down or even prevent long-term healing. Whatever underlying emotion you've been desperately trying to avoid remains because it hasn't been addressed.

Before I learned the Emotional Alchemy process, I was afraid that if I let myself feel my emotions they would be all-consuming. My fear was that I would get stuck in my sadness or anxiety and it would never go away. This fear is exactly why most people spend their whole life avoiding their feelings—until they can't keep stuffing them down anymore. At some point or another, suppressed emotions will come to the surface to be processed and released.

Perhaps this is where you are right now. Maybe you're so tired of feeling sad, anxious, or empty inside that you're ready to give up all of your old coping mechanisms and try a different approach. Or maybe your relationships at home or work have reached a critical point, and you know it will all fall apart if something doesn't change.

Wherever you are, I promise that the fastest way to break through is to courageously learn how to feel your emotions. If you really want to heal the emotional pain you've been carrying, you must be willing to feel the emotions you've been avoiding. As Emily Nagoski, the author of *Come As You Are,* says, "Emotions are tunnels. You have to go all the way through the darkness to get to the light at the end."[5] In other words, the only way out is through.

Jenna's Emotional Alchemy Journey

In 2021, in the midst of the Covid-19 pandemic, Jenna found herself struggling with anxiety on a daily basis. For months she would wake up with her heart racing and couldn't get through a day without feeling on edge. She went to therapy every week, took yoga classes, and tried various meditation and journaling techniques to navigate her anxiety, but nothing was working. After listening to an episode of the Feminine Frequency podcast, Jenna knew it was time to try something new, and reached out to me for support.

During our first few sessions, we focused on techniques to help her ground her nervous system. Once she learned how to regulate her nervous system during moments of panic and emotional discomfort, we were able to go deeper to explore the root cause of her debilitating anxiety. I guided her through a deep embodiment visualization to explore the sensations of the anxiety she was feeling in her body. During this practice, we created a safe space for her to get curious about the sensations and what her anxiety was trying to tell her. Through subconscious exploration, she was able to identify a childhood experience where she felt abandoned by a male figure in her life. Now, as an adult, every time she felt like she couldn't trust her romantic partner or had a fear that their relationship might end, it brought her back to the traumatic experience in her childhood when her father neglected to follow through with his promises.

Over the next six months, Jenna learned how to honor the emotional pain she experienced during her childhood. Whenever she felt afraid or unlovable, she would pause, go within, and nurture her inner child. As she learned to honor her emotions, she was able to meet her anxiety with compassion and understanding. When her anxiety came back for a visit, she knew exactly how to move the energy through her body and was able to come back to a calm, grounded state quickly.

From this empowered emotional state, Jenna was able to articulate her feelings to her romantic partner as they arose, instead of being reactive or projecting her past pain onto him. This led to deeper intimacy, connection, and trust in their relationship. Jenna recently shared that their relationship has never been stronger and that they were now planning to move in together. All of this was possible because she was courageous enough to go through the Emotional Alchemy process and look at the deeper emotional wounds that were asking for her attention.

Emotional Release Ritual

The practice we'll be using to alchemize your emotions is called a "release ritual." It's a sacred healing practice designed to help you come back into alignment with your natural state of love and inner peace.

Remember, if this work feels like too much to handle on your own, be sure to seek professional support from a therapist or a qualified coach before diving in.

Step 1: Set your environment

- Find a space where you know you'll be uninterrupted and aren't worried about other people hearing or seeing you.
- Pick a time of day where you don't feel rushed.
- For your first session, set a timer for twenty minutes.

Step 2: Reignite your emotions

- Put on a "feeling" playlist that matches the energy of the emotions you're trying to release.
- Write in your journal about anything that's frustrating, upsetting, or triggering you.
- Visualize a situation where you felt triggered or frustrated.
- Pay attention to any sensations that arise in your body such as tightness, tingling, heaviness, clenching, or heat.

Step 3: Release

- Let yourself cry, scream, shake, punch a pillow, and/or stomp your feet. Let your body, not your logical mind, guide your actions. If you feel like you're pushing your emotions away or judging them, keep coming back to your breath and reconnect to the sensations in your body.
- Keep letting the emotions flow until you feel like you've felt it all the way through.
- Note: Sometimes, after you feel one emotion, like anger, another deeper emotion, like sadness, may arise. This is totally normal and is a positive sign that you're moving through all of the layers.

Step 4: Recalibrate: Ground your nervous system

- Give yourself a hug.
- Repeat "I'm safe" or "It's safe for me to feel this" out loud.
- Take slow, deep breaths.
- Bring your attention to any part of your body that's touching the ground.

Step 5: Reflect

- Notice how you're feeling now that the emotions have moved through.
- Write in your journal about your experience.
- Ask yourself if there's anything you need before you move on to the next part of your day.

The Breakdown Before the Breakthrough

It's a courageous act to be willing to explore the depths of your emotions and allow yourself to feel in this way. And while in the moment it might feel like the emotional turmoil you're experiencing is going to last forever, I assure you that's not the case. Whenever we're faced with darkness, there's always light waiting for us on the other side. As many spiritual teachers have shared, after every breakdown there's a breakthrough.

On the other side of the release process is a whole new discovery of freedom, joy, and pleasure. As we let go of the denser energies and trapped emotions from our body and energetic field, we create space for clarity, peace, and empowerment.

Walking the path of the Feminine allows for all of life to move through you—including the full spectrum of pleasure, pain, and everything in between. This is what it means to be fully alive. And in the next chapter, we'll be exploring how to invite new levels of pleasure and aliveness into your everyday life.

Soul Reflections

- What did your parents, teachers, friends, and community teach you about your emotions when you were younger?
- How do you currently relate to your emotions when they come up?
- Are there any numbing or distraction methods you use to avoid your emotions?
- Is there any past pain, hurt, or resentment you feel like you're still holding onto?
- What do you feel your "heavier" emotions (anxiety, sadness, fear, shame, grief, etc.) are trying to teach you right now?
- What does your inner child need to hear when you experience challenging emotions?

"So many of us were taught to keep a lid on anything and everything outrageous. To just turn it off. We turn off our life force, turn off our feelings, turn off our sensuality, and as a consequence, we turn off our power."

Regena Thomashauer

chapter six

Prioritizing Pleasure

"Where did you get this? And how did I not know about it?"

My mom was standing in my room with a disconcerted look on her face. I followed her gaze to the package of birth control I'd left open on my bed, and I immediately felt my body temperature increase as a heavy feeling of shame washed over me.

When I didn't respond, she followed up with more questions. "How long have you been taking this? Why didn't you tell me about this? What if something happened to you?"

I could feel her concern and discomfort filling the room as she waited for me to speak. Time moved in slow motion. It felt like forever before I could find the right words. Frantically, I tried to think of an excuse for why I would be secretly taking birth control, but it was obvious I was hiding it for a reason. The energy of disappointment and shame continued to fill my body as I spilled the truth: I was sexually active, and now it was impossible for me to deny it.

Growing up in a traditional, religious home, sex was not something we talked about. There was an unspoken narrative that sex was inappropriate, and in my mind, this meant that sex was bad—and, more specifically, that *I* was bad if I was having sex. This wasn't my parents' fault. They were worried about me and trying to protect me the best way they knew how. Although they were just trying to keep me safe, the message I internalized was, ultimately, not a positive one.

From a young age, I remember being naturally curious about sex. I was open to exploring my sexuality, yet at the same time I felt like I needed to hide this part of myself for fear of getting in trouble. It felt like I was living a double life where I was pretending to be the innocent "Good Girl" to gain the approval of my parents, but at the same time was hungry to explore my sexual curiosities. I carried this pattern of shame around my sexuality with me through my teenage years.

Once I got to college, I felt more freedom to explore my sexuality without the fear of my parents finding out. But I was still afraid of being judged by others for being "slutty" or promiscuous. It wasn't until almost a decade later, after I went through my spiritual awakening and got divorced, that I started to do some deeper healing work around my sexuality. I realized that the sexual shame I'd been carrying was blocking me from experiencing pleasure to my fullest capacity. Throughout my twenties, I remember being embarrassed to talk about sex, or to even say the word "orgasm" out loud.

As I started to dissolve the shame around my sexuality, I got curious about my own pleasure. I realized that, up until this point, sex had never been focused on *my* pleasure; it had always been about pleasing my partner. Once this became clear, I recognized that it was time to reclaim my pleasure and completely rewire my relationship with sex. My sexual awakening had begun, and I was thirsty to get my hands on all of the books and knowledge I could to learn more about female pleasure.

I dove into the world of sacred sexuality and tantra where I learned about using yoni eggs, crystal wands, and my own breath to activate more pleasure in my body. It felt as though my eyes had been opened to a whole new realm of pleasure, one that had been hidden from me for my whole life.

Becoming more empowered with my own pleasure took the quality of sex with my romantic partner to a whole new level. Instead of focusing on how my body looked or wondering if my partner was enjoying what I was doing, I was able to relax into the moment. The more I was able to get out of my mind, the more I could truly feel in my body ... and the change was sensational. During my next intimate experience, as my partner's fingertips traced slowly on my skin, I could feel aliveness waking up within me. My breathing slowed down, my lips softly parted, and I felt sexual energy coursing through me. He could feel my body relax and could sense how much pleasure his soft caress was bringing to my body. My receptivity to his touch led to him feeling even more turned on, and the sexual energy between us continued to build. The sensations of my orgasmic energy were like nothing I'd ever felt before.

Another huge shift I noticed as a result of this inner work around my own pleasure was my confidence to communicate my desires and my boundaries both inside and outside of the bedroom. Instead of pretending that everything my partner was doing felt good, I was able to ask for what I wanted and direct him to the areas of my body that brought me the most pleasure. This not only allowed me to receive more pleasure, but it also inspired my partner to focus on giving me more pleasure because he could tell how much I was enjoying it.

The heightened level of pleasure I was experiencing within myself and with my partner didn't stop in the bedroom. As I reconnected with my pleasure, I felt my aliveness, my Feminine power, my creativity, and my confidence come online in my business and my everyday life. I noticed a deeper connection to my body. I felt more magnetic, more self-expressed, and I was able to experience more pleasure in the small moments throughout my day. Even though I've come a long way, I know there are even deeper layers of orgasmic pleasure for me to uncover.

Similar to the other Feminine Codes we've covered so far, the Code of Prioritizing Pleasure is an ongoing, many-layered practice. In this chapter, I'm excited to take you on a journey of reclaiming your pleasure through dissolving shame, awakening your sensuality, and infusing aliveness into all aspects of your life.

Shall we?

The Pleasure Revolution

After centuries of sexual suppression due to toxic religious and patriarchal programming, women are starting to reawaken their connection to their Feminine desire for pleasure both inside and outside of the bedroom. The days of operating from pressure, performance, and self-sacrifice are coming to an end.

For far too long we've been told that, in order to be a good woman/daughter/wife/mother, we should set aside our own need for pleasure and enjoyment, and instead focus on other people's needs and expectations. This lack of prioritizing pleasure has left women feeling dry, hollow, and parched. On one end of the spectrum, we see women who are simply going through the motions, feeling lethargic, uninspired, and bored throughout their days. On the other end, we see women hustling like their male counterparts to prove their worth and climb the ladder, which leaves them feeling stressed out, overwhelmed, and depleted. After putting pleasure at the bottom of our collective to-do list for so long, is it any wonder that over twelve million women experience clinical depression each year, or that 50 percent of women report experiencing burnout each year?[6] When a woman is disconnected from her natural essence of pleasure, it makes sense that she might struggle to show up as her most vibrant and alive self.

One major reason why women deprioritize or even demonize pleasure is because of internalized sexual shame. The effects of sexual shame aren't limited to our encounters with our partners;

they can extend far beyond the bedroom. When women feel shame around their sexuality, we also experience shame around our body image, what we wear, how we interact with men, or even how we feel when we walk down the street. Without consciously realizing the source, we might feel uncomfortable, inappropriate, or embarrassed for enjoying things like certain physical movements when working out, dancing, or doing yoga, and not realize where those feelings come from. Sexual shame is often buried deep within us, but once we uncover it, we can finally see just how much it affects our daily lives.

Hyper-productivity and the expectation that women can and should "do it all" isn't the only source of our aversion to pleasure. Cultural traditions and religious institutions often contribute to this as well. Many of us grew up in religious environments that hold toxic views around pleasure and sexuality. We've been taught by religion that the purpose of sex is procreation within marriage, and that having sex outside of that context is wrong, inappropriate, or dirty.

Interestingly, while some religious teachings drive women to feel shame around their sexuality, they have also birthed a whole industry and culture of women's bodies being hyper-sexualized and objectified through pornography, media, and advertisements. We're naturally drawn to the forbidden, and sex is no exception. This patriarchal viewpoint, when distilled to its essence, teaches that sex is intended to provide pleasure and enjoyment for men. Our sexuality is treated as a commodity to be sought after, "preserved" for marriage, and then enjoyed at our partners' discretion.

In addition to religious and cultural programming, many women also carry shame from sexual trauma. According to the 2015 National Intimate Partner and Sexual Violence Survey, conducted by the CDC's National Center for Injury Prevention and Control, one in five women in the United States have reported experiencing sexual abuse at some point in their life.[7] It's no wonder women feel so disconnected from their own pleasure and desires!

If we could take a step back and remove all of the toxic narratives and traumatic experiences around pleasure that have been imprinted within and around us, we would see that *there is absolutely nothing wrong with a woman's desire to experience pleasure.* These narratives have been put in place, in part, as a method to control women—because when a woman is connected to her pleasure, she's powerful beyond measure. Before the Piscean Age, when our views around sexuality became tainted with religious programming, women's pleasure and sexuality was regarded by many cultures as sacred and holy. This is the truth that we're in the process of remembering as individuals and as a collective.

As you move through your own journey of peeling back the layers of shame and/or trauma you've experienced, you'll discover that your desire for pleasure is pure and innocent. At your core, you're a spiritual being designed to receive and share pleasure, because that's the nature of the Feminine.

If you desire to live in a more fully expressed way and to reclaim your aliveness and Feminine flow, it's time to release any internalized shame and reclaim your sovereignty as a woman who's empowered in her sexuality.

The Pleasure Revolution

We're in the midst of a pleasure revolution, and it's just getting started.

Despite centuries of messaging to the contrary, women today are waking up to their innate desire for pleasure, questioning the messaging they've internalized around pleasure and sexuality, and speaking openly about this formerly taboo topic. By doing so, they're leading other women out of the darkness of shame and into the light of radiant Feminine pleasure.

Pleasure is our birthright. It's a natural part of us, and it's a key ingredient to experiencing joy, fulfillment, and purpose in our lives.

When a woman is connected to her pleasure, she's connected to her life force energy. Through pleasure, she opens the doorway to her creativity, abundance, and Feminine power. A woman who's connected to her pleasure is connected to her desires, both inside and outside the bedroom; she knows what she likes, she knows what feels good, and she no longer needs to look to other people's opinions to make decisions. She can feel her true "Yes" and her true "No"—and she can no longer be shamed into letting down her boundaries just to make other people happy. Pleasure becomes her barometer in how she navigates the world. Instead of making decisions from a place of guilt, fear, and shame, she now seeks the people, situations, and experiences that bring her the most pleasure—the things that light her up and turn her on.

Imagine how much more she would enjoy her life, instead of just going through the motions. Imagine how everyone else—her partner, coworkers, kids, even total strangers she interacts with in passing—would benefit from her being turned on to life. Imagine how much more happiness, creativity, and inspiration would be brought into the world!

Reconnecting to pleasure is about awakening to authentic aliveness, and it changes everything. When a woman is connected to her pleasure, everyone wins.

Replacing Pressure with Pleasure

Up until now, it's likely that most of your adult life (and maybe even your childhood) has been motivated by the pressure others have put upon you, and that you've put upon yourself. The pressure to get good grades, be successful, look pretty, have the perfect body, and be nice to everyone is, to be frank, *freaking exhausting*. Every time you say yes to doing things you don't want to do, it takes you one step further away from creating the pleasure-filled life you desire.

What if, instead of spending your precious time and energy doing things to make other people happy, you decided to focus only on activities and experiences that make you feel good? What if instead of eating bland and tasteless foods that are supposed to make you lose weight, you allowed yourself to eat foods that tasted delicious and that you really enjoyed? What if instead of doing workouts that you dread, you started taking walks outside in nature, or found a different workout that you actually looked forward to? What if instead of saying yes to every social invitation, you only said yes to the people and activities you truly enjoy?

When you reclaim your right to experience pleasure, you can create a life that turns you on. After all, you only have this one life to live, so why not make it the best and most enjoyable life you can?

From a Masculine standpoint, pressure is a good motivator. It's inherent to a goal-oriented approach. However, when we take this approach, we're often so focused on the end goal that we forget to enjoy the process, and end up feeling empty and flat. If you can relate to putting pressure on yourself to overperform in your life, your inner Feminine is likely thirsty for the feeling of aliveness. Your Soul didn't come here to go through the motions, check things off the list, and just "get through the day." You came here to taste the nectar of life—to experience delicious pleasure, joy, and fulfillment. If your goals aren't doing that for you, it's time to try a new approach.

Pleasure Inventory

Have you ever stopped to think about what actually brings you pleasure?

When I first started orienting my life toward pleasure, it felt really challenging for me to come up with a list of even five activities or experiences that brought me pleasure. I'd been living out of "should" for so long that I had no idea what I actually enjoyed!

Remember, when I'm talking about pleasure, I'm not exclusively referring to sexual pleasure. Sensual pleasure can be experienced in the moments where you pause to take a deep, nourishing breath, when you smell a beautiful flower, or when put on a warm and cozy sweater. Any time you can tap into the sensations of taste, touch, sound, smell, or sight, you have the opportunity to experience a pleasurable moment.

Now that we're clear on the various types of pleasure, it's time to come up with your own pleasure inventory.

Write down a list of ten to fifteen activities or experiences that bring you pleasure.

Here are some of my examples:

- Getting into bed with clean sheets.
- A warm matcha latte in the morning.
- Watching a beautiful sunset.
- Receiving a massage or any form of loving touch.
- Taking a bite of a delicious piece of fruit.
- Reading a fiction book at a coffee shop.
- Laying in nature with the warm sun on my skin.
- Curling up on the couch with a warm, fuzzy blanket.

Now it's your turn. Get out your journal and make your list. If you're not sure, keep it simple. Or write down some activities you think would bring you pleasure but that you haven't tried yet!

Awakening Sensual Pleasure

No matter how disconnected you feel from your Feminine pleasure right now, it's 100 percent possible to reawaken your sensuality through simple mindfulness and embodiment practices. With loving awareness and patience, we can thaw out the numbness and bring the sensations of pleasure back to life.

In order to awaken more pleasure, you must learn how to slow down and tune into the sensations that your body is receiving on a moment-to-moment basis. As humans, our five senses are the mechanism through which we connect with pleasure. Our senses cannot be felt in our minds; they can only be felt through the body. This means that if you want to experience more pleasure in your everyday life, you'll need to practice being more present with your senses.

While your mind is constantly using your five senses of smell, taste, touch, sound, and sight to take in the world around you, these sensory inputs are often on autopilot—meaning that your subconscious mind is going through the motions and taking in information, but you're not actually feeling, enjoying, or responding to the sensations you're experiencing. For example, when you go to a restaurant and you're on autopilot, you take a bite of food, chew, and swallow, but that doesn't mean you're actually tasting the flavors of the food. Your senses are still working, because if you didn't like the taste you'd know it and would likely stop eating. Similarly, if the food was too hot, your senses would notify you and you would wait until your food cooled down to eat it. Even though you're cognitively using your senses, it doesn't mean you're consciously connected to them, or that you're receiving pleasure from your food.

So, what does it look like to intentionally connect to your senses in a way that helps you to experience more pleasure? Imagine you're at the same restaurant and you've ordered the same dish—except this time, before you start eating, you slow down to take a few deep breaths, look at the colors of your food, take in the delicious aroma, and feel gratitude that you get to eat this amazing meal. Then, as you slowly chew every bite, you notice the symphony of flavors, and let each rest on your tastebuds before you swallow and take a new bite. Your body may even let out a little moan of delight because this food tastes and feels so delightful.

The more you intentionally connect to your senses, the easier it will become to access your pleasure pathways, and the more pleasure you'll start to experience throughout your day.

In the following meditation, we'll practice awakening your senses and reconnecting with your innate sensual essence.

Awakening Your Senses Meditation

1. Find a comfortable place to sit without any distractions. Sitting outside in nature will enhance your experience, but you can also do this indoors.

2. Gently close your eyes and set your intention to connect more deeply with pleasure in your body.
3. Take three deep, slow breaths. As you breathe, pay attention to how your body expands on the inhales and relaxes on the exhales.
4. Bring your awareness to the sensation of touch. Notice the texture of your clothing on your skin. If it feels good, you can gently run your fingertips down your arms and feel the sensation on your skin. Take a deep breath in and out of your body.
5. Bring your awareness to any scents that you smell around you. Perhaps it's the smell of fresh cut grass, a candle, or the scent of your body lotion. Take a deep breath in and out of your body.
6. Bring your awareness to your eyesight. Notice if there are any colors or patterns you can see behind your eyelids. Take a deep breath in and out of your body.
7. Bring your awareness to the taste in your mouth. Bring to mind the flavors of something delicious that you've tasted recently. Take a deep breath in and out of your body.
8. Bring your awareness to your ears and to any sounds you can hear. Maybe you can hear the rustle of the wind in the trees, or the sound of music in the background. Take a deep breath in and out of your body.

9. Once you've explored all of your five senses, take a gentle stretch and come back into your day.

You'll find an audio version of this meditation at www.amynatalieco.com/bookresources.

As you begin to become more present with your senses, you'll start to notice the little moments throughout the day where you could allow yourself to experience more pleasure. Perhaps it's slowing down to really taste the flavor of a hot morning beverage, or feeling the sensation of the wind as it sweeps across your skin. Maybe it's pausing to enjoy the sound of the music you're listening to, or to take in the feeling of grass on your bare feet. It's in these little moments where you can practice opening to more pleasure and aliveness.

Kate's Pleasure Journey

Kate came to me feeling depressed, lost, and confused. After having three kids and working a full-time job, she'd lost touch with herself. Prior to having kids, Kate remembers being passionate about life, having fun, and enjoying her sex life with her husband. She deeply wanted to reconnect with her spark, and get back to the playful and alive version of herself.

After listening to the Feminine Frequency podcast for almost a year, she realized she'd been operating in Masculine overdrive for way too long. Kate felt overwhelmed, exhausted, and completely disinterested in having sex with her husband. She shared, "These past five years have been focused on giving to everyone else in my life, taking care of my family, and keeping my house in order. I didn't realize that I've been completely neglecting my self-care. I feel like I lost myself somewhere along the way. I have to make a change. I can't keep on going like this."

When Kate finally reached out for support, she was fully committed to making a change. We started infusing the Feminine Codes of Deepening Devotion, Awakening Intuition, and Emotional Alchemy into her life. Over the next few months, she started to regain her vitality. She was no longer operating in survival mode.

But our work wasn't done. Kate wasn't just looking to get out of survival mode, she was devoted to creating a life where she was thriving in all aspects of her being. Now that she had more energy, she was ready to go deeper. It was time to dive into the world of Feminine pleasure.

First, we curated a list of small daily experiences that would support her in infusing more pleasure into her life—like going to a coffee shop by herself to read a book, spending time in nature, and soaking in a warm bubble bath at least once a week. Then, we explored the realm of self-touch and connecting with her own sensuality. And finally, we played with inviting more passion and physical intimacy into her sex life with her husband.

By the end of our work together, Kate didn't even look like the same woman I'd met six months prior. Her skin was glowing, her face looked relaxed, and her body oozed sensuality and aliveness. She was turned on to life. Through reconnecting with her own pleasure, she was able to be more present with her kids and actually enjoyed coming up with fun ideas to engage with them. She finally had the energy to reach out to other moms and start making friends again. For the first time in years, she felt inspired to start a new art project and focus on hobbies that brought her joy. And, finally, she felt the spark come back in her relationship with her husband; instead of just going through the motions, they were having fun exploring together in the bedroom.

So far in this chapter we've been focused on awakening your sensuality and pleasure in non-sexual moments. The next step on your pleasure journey is learning how to reconnect with your Shakti energy to awaken your sexual energy.

I want to note that the process of connecting with your sacred Feminine energy and awakening pleasure in your body is, first and foremost, for you. Experiencing more pleasure with a partner is a secondary benefit, and it's not necessary for this practice. Whether you're currently partnered or not, as you begin to reclaim your pleasure in this way, you're opening the channel for more pleasure, creativity, and abundance in all areas of your life.

Awakening Shakti Energy

In the Hindu tradition, Shakti is known as the goddess of creation and Feminine energy. For this reason, Shakti energy is a powerful force that's responsible for the creation of all of life. Awakening your Shakti energy is the key to activating your primal life force energy, also known as your sexual energy.

Your Shakti energy is said to live at the base of your spine and is depicted as a coiled snake. As you go through your Feminine awakening, this energy starts traveling up your spine and moves through your body, activating each of your seven chakras as it goes. In particular, your sacral (second) chakra is associated with awakening your sensual and creative powers; this energy center is located just below your belly button in your womb space. You can start to wake up your Shakti energy by simply bringing awareness, breath, and movement to this area of your body.

Awakening Shakti Practice

Here's a sample practice to get you started:

- Standing with your feet slightly apart, bring both hands to your sacral chakra, just below your navel, and take a few deep breaths into this space.
- Once you feel comfortable here, invite some gentle movement into your hips by rotating them in a circular motion. This movement can be small and subtle

at first, or you can start to make the circles bigger, moving in one direction for five to ten circles and then moving in the other direction for five to ten circles.

- As you move your hips in circles, stay connected to your breath and notice any sensations in your body. At first you'll likely notice some tightness or tension you've been carrying in your hips. Keep moving your hips gently and you'll notice sensations of pleasure and "turn-on" starting to arise.

If you don't feel anything the first time, keep coming back to this practice every day, as sometimes it takes time to awaken this energy if the volume has been turned down for a while.

You can also do this practice on the ground by getting onto all fours with your knees and the palms of your hands touching the earth. From this position, you can move in the "cat-cow" yoga pose, alternating between puffing up the top of your shoulders as you round your spine and looking toward your belly button and arching your spine and looking upward. As you move between these two poses of extension and flexion, use your breath to guide you—focusing on the exhale when you round your back and the inhale when you arch your back. When you feel comfortable with this motion, you can start moving your hips and your spine in a circular motion in whatever way feels good to you. It doesn't matter how this looks or if you're doing it perfectly. The most important thing is to focus on how it feels in your body. As you move your hips in circles, notice if it feels good to let out a pleasurable sound on your exhale. By now, you'll likely feel your Shakti energy in your sacral region—it could feel like a delicious buzzing or pulsing sensation—or you might even feel a pleasurable sensation moving throughout your entire body. Keep breathing and moving until you feel complete with this practice.

Understanding Female Arousal

Growing up, most women (and men) receive very little education about female pleasure. In middle school, you may have sat through an awkward sex education class that focused mainly on how to prevent pregnancy and avoid STIs. And as a young adult, it's likely you learned about sex through watching pornography or R-rated movies, or by reading racy magazines—all of which are completely performative and misleading when it comes to how female pleasure and orgasm works.

It's no wonder why so many women share that they feel dissatisfied or disinterested in having sex. A 2017 study on orgasm frequency published in *Archives of Sexual Behavior* found that while 95 percent of heterosexual men usually or always orgasmed during sex, only 65 percent of heterosexual women could say the same.[8] Additionally, the study found that approximately 10 percent of women surveyed had never experienced an orgasm before. While these statistics are unfortunate and unfavorable, as a woman they're not a prediction of your future. You have the power and the right to become more educated about your own pleasure through learning about female anatomy and understanding your own body.

You may be surprised to learn that on average it takes a woman thirty to forty minutes to become fully aroused, and that 81.6 percent of women aren't able to have an orgasm through sexual penetration alone.[9] In her book, *Women's Anatomy of Arousal,* Sheri Winston writes about how the lack of sexual education and misinformation about a woman's pleasure often leads to women feeling like there's something wrong with them or like they're "broken," when in reality neither men nor women have been taught how female arousal actually works. She writes: "Sexually challenged people may go through life feeling broken, and possibly damaged beyond repair. Some repress their sexuality and channel the energy elsewhere. Others pretend they just don't care ("It's okay, I don't mind if I don't come.") Some people carry their shame in plain view while desperately trying to hide it. Others successfully keep their problems in the closet."[10]

One of the biggest mistakes women make when trying to experience more pleasure is that we take a goal-oriented approach to our sexual experiences, where the focus is purely on reaching a climax and having an orgasm. This Masculine approach to sexuality makes it challenging to be present in your body and neglects all of the delightful and pleasurable sensations that can be experienced with or without an orgasm. The more you're able to relax into your Feminine, connect to your breath, and feel the sensations in your body, without forcing or rushing the process, the more pleasure you will feel along the way, and ironically, the higher the chances that you'll be able to experience an orgasm—or even multiple orgasms.

If you're wanting to open to deeper levels of pleasure with a partner, it starts with opening to deeper intimacy and pleasure with yourself. Taking time to get to know your body, what feels good to you, and what doesn't feel good is the key to reclaiming your pleasure and being able to ask for what you want from your partner.

Cultivating deeper intimacy with yourself doesn't happen overnight. Be patient with yourself as you continue to show up with devotion to your own self-pleasure practice. If you've never journeyed into self-pleasure, the ritual below is a great starting point. Alternatively, if you already have a self-pleasure practice, create space this week to connect with your body and your pleasure.

Note: Many women are used to relying on using a vibrator to give themselves pleasure—however, there are other self-pleasure tools that can be incorporated to increase pleasure and arousal such as yoni eggs and crystal pleasure wands. See the resources section for recommendations on self-pleasure tools at www.amynatalieco.com/bookresources.

Self-Pleasure Ritual

1. Set up a sacred space. Turn the lights down, light some candles, and turn on some sensual music.
2. Depending on your comfort level, you may choose to wear loose clothing or sexy lingerie for this ritual, or you can be naked.

3. Take five to ten slow, nourishing breaths to connect with your body.
4. Start to explore your own body with gentle touch or self-massage. I encourage you to use lotion or body oil for this. Massage around your breasts, your belly, your arms, and your thighs.
5. If it feels good, you can start to bring some movement into your pelvis by rolling your hips around in circles while staying connected to your breath.
6. When you feel ready, start to explore your outer labia with your fingers first. Massage around the outside of your vaginal opening on your clitoris, working your way down the clitoral shaft on both sides.
7. Check in with yourself to see if you feel ready for internal penetration with either your fingers or with a crystal wand. Remember, take your time here; there's no rush. If you notice any shame arising, pause and breathe through the emotion and/or discomfort. You can always go back to gentle self-touch in other areas of your body.
8. Continue to massage or touch your clitoris while you explore the inside of your vagina with the wand or your fingers. Use your breath to stay connected to the sensations of pleasure you're experiencing. If it feels good to make any sounds/noises while different sensations arise, allow yourself to express freely.

9. When you feel complete or when you reach orgasm, notice if any emotions arise in your body. Be gentle with whatever is present and breathe through it. Give yourself a hug to complete your practice.

As you become more comfortable with self-pleasure, you will notice your relationship with your body and your confidence continuing to deepen. Be patient with the process of awakening pleasure in your body as there are many energetic and emotional layers to work through as you open yourself to access more pleasure.

Enhancing Sexual Polarity

We covered the basics of Energetic Polarity in Chapter Two. Now let's look at how they can play out when it comes to sensuality and desire.

When Masculine and Feminine energies are out of balance within a relationship, it can often lead to a lack of desire for pleasure, and to diminished sexual intimacy. One of the fastest ways to bring that spark back is to intentionally bring more polarity into the relationship. Understanding the nature of Energetic Polarity is essential for activating more chemistry in the dynamic between you and your partner. But what does this look like in practice?

Just like a magnet, in order for there to be chemistry between two people, one person must hold the Masculine energetic charge and the other person must hold the Feminine energetic charge. If both people are holding a Masculine charge, tension or competition often arises, or the two people end up functioning more like business partners rather than lovers. On the other end of the spectrum, if both people are in their Feminine essence, it can feel more like a roommate or "bestie" situation.

Many women today operate in their Masculine energy of organizing, completing tasks, and meeting goals and deadlines at work and/or in caretaking their children and household. Often, women will carry their Masculine energy over into their relationships, which may not lend itself to maintaining sexual polarity with their partners. In some cases, when a woman is dominant in her Masculine energy, it pushes her partner into their Feminine energetic state, in which they don't have the opportunity to take the lead or make decisions. In other cases, it causes conflict and arguments because there's a power struggle between the two partners.

One of the fastest ways to de-escalate this issue and to repolarize a relationship is for both partners to understand the nature of polarity and to learn how to shift between Masculine and Feminine energy within themselves. For a woman, this can look like learning how to connect to her body and her pleasure instead of continuing in "doing, planning, controlling, and thinking" mode. When she consciously chooses to relax into her Feminine energy, it naturally encourages her partner to step forward in their Masculine energy of leading, taking action, and penetrating.

In my coaching practice, many women come to me saying, "I want my partner to show up more in their Masculine energy." The reality is, if you want your partner to step into their Masculine energy more, you must create space for them to do so. Ambitious women who are used to making things happen at work can easily carry this energy into their romantic relationships. However, when you're constantly planning, controlling, and demanding, your partner has no opportunity to take the lead. Simply put, what works for you in the boardroom is not always going to work for you in the bedroom.

It's important to note here that this isn't about becoming more "submissive," "ladylike," or even "feminine" in the traditional sense of the word. You don't have to diminish yourself or ignore your personal preferences to satisfy your partner or create sexual polarity in your relationship. Instead, you're being offered an opportunity to explore your Masculine and Feminine energies and create a relationship dynamic that feels fulfilling and enlivening.

Let's look at a real-life example. Picture this: you've just come home from a busy day at work and your mind is racing with all the things you need to do. You're still in "get shit done" mode, checking off your mental to-do list, when your partner walks through the door. As your partner hugs you and says hello, your mind is still occupied by all of the things you need to get done. You continue in "doing" mode through dinner and beyond, and by the bedtime you're exhausted. Your partner tries to initiate sex, but it's the last thing you want to do. You tell them you're too tired—or, you say yes and spend the next thirty minutes waiting for it to be over.

If this sounds like you, imagine this instead: at the end of your busy day, before your partner gets home, you take a few deep breaths, have a dance party in your car, go for a short walk, or step outside into nature and put your feet in the grass. Within a few minutes, your energy has traveled from your mind back into your heart and you feel more relaxed, open, and receptive. When your partner comes home from work, they feel something is different. As they wrap their arms around you, you melt and soften into their embrace. You notice you feel less on edge and more at ease as you flow into your evening together. As you move around your space, you feel their presence and their desire for you, which in turn makes you feel a desire for deeper intimacy and connection.

Making the effort to shift out of your Masculine energy before spending time with your partner not only supports you to feel at ease and connected to your own pleasure, but it also creates an opportunity for more emotional and physical intimacy. It's important to note that these changes take time; you won't master these inner polarity shifts overnight. However, the more mindful you are about your inner polarity and the more you master the art of flowing between your Masculine and Feminine energy, the more positive shifts you'll notice within your relationship.

Pleasure Integration

In this chapter, we've explored the benefits of prioritizing pleasure in your everyday life, in your self-pleasure practice, and within your romantic relationships. Your devotion to pleasure and aliveness will benefit you in all areas of your life. As you continue to infuse pleasure into your everyday routines, you'll begin to experience more creativity, ease, and confidence. You may even find that, with your newfound aliveness, radiance, and turn-on, you're inspired to pour this enhanced energy and Feminine flow into a passion project, creative endeavor, or even a new business.

In the next chapter, we'll be exploring the Feminine Code of Soul Calling—otherwise known as your purpose—and magnetizing abundance through your unique gifts. What if I told you that your life's work could be pleasurable instead of stressful, and that you can make good money doing work you enjoy and are passionate about?

Let's continue!

Soul Reflections

- What messages did you receive from your parents, religion, or society about sex and pleasure when you were younger?
- Have you had any sexual experiences in your life that have contributed to feeling shame around pleasure and sexuality?
- How do you currently feel about your relationship with sex and pleasure?
- What do you feel will be different in your life as you begin to prioritize more pleasure?

"Lightworkers are here to grow as individuals and also to contribute to the planet in some action-oriented way. Their Soul mission is often answered through a career calling or by devoting their life to something bigger."

Rebecca Campbell

chapter seven

Soul Calling

After graduating with my undergraduate degree in Business Administration, I had no idea what I wanted to do next. I moved back in with my parents and started working as a hostess at a local restaurant. Even though I enjoyed the people I worked with, I very quickly realized that I wasn't feeling fulfilled by how I was spending my time.

I knew I wanted to do something I was passionate about. I also knew I didn't want to work a nine-to-five job. "What's my purpose?" I wondered. "What do I want to do with my life? Why am I here?" I wanted to have the freedom to make my own schedule, and I wanted to make a difference in the lives of other people. But I had no idea what work like that could look like.

After going through my personal health challenges and receiving a tremendous amount of value from working with a local nutritionist, I decided I wanted to study nutrition so I could empower others with their own health and well-being. One night while browsing on the internet, I discovered a health coaching certification program and felt a deep resonance with the path of becoming a coach and a mentor. The idea of teaching, supporting, and guiding others felt exciting and fulfilling. I was ready to go back to school, but this time to learn something I was deeply passionate about.

Once I'd received my certifications as a clinical nutritionist and a holistic health coach, I was excited to start working with clients. Little did I know that following my Soul Calling and beginning my path as a Soulpreneur—a heart-centered, mission-led entrepreneur—would invite me into a deep personal growth journey. As I launched my in-person nutrition practice, I soon found that all of my insecurities, doubts, and fears came to the surface.

For the first two years of my business, I tried to figure it all out on my own: the fear of judgment, imposter syndrome, and deep scarcity mindset. Eventually, I realized that what I was doing—hosting one-off workshops, attending networking events, and charging too little for my services—was not sustainable. I hired a business coach, but even with the right business strategies in place, fears and negative self-talk persisted.

In order to overcome my inner resistance, I recognized there was some inner healing that needed to be done. This was right around the time I was contemplating divorce, struggling with depression and emotional eating, and questioning many of my life choices. Something had to change.

After hitting my rock bottom and finding my spiritual path, I started studying mindset work, manifestation, and healing my childhood wounds. The more I applied daily Feminine practices and spiritual rituals to my life, the faster I started to see results in my health, my relationships, and my business. I started applying these techniques in my work with clients, and they too received better results—not only with their health goals, but in all areas of their lives. Eventually, I felt so inspired by the results that both myself and my clients were getting that I realized I had a deeper calling than nutrition and health coaching alone.

Over the next year, I slowly transitioned my coaching practice to focus on empowering women to listen to their intuition, to elevate their confidence, and to align with their purpose. It was terrifying to take the leap and completely let go of my nutrition business, but my Soul knew that this deeper transformational work was exactly what I came here to do. This was the turning point where I was ready to fully embody my Soul mission. From this place, I started attracting my Soul clients—women who were ready to do the deeper work, and who were a perfect match for the wisdom I had to offer. As I saw women's lives transforming before my eyes, I'd never felt so much fulfillment from the work I was doing. All I wanted was to grow my business and serve more women around the world.

At this point, I hired another business coach. Over the next year, my income doubled. I was implementing all of the systems and strategies I was learning, showing up consistently, and getting the results I'd always dreamed of.

The problem was, after a year of being hyper-focused on scaling my business, I realized that I felt disconnected from the joy and passion that had inspired me in the first place. I was tired, uninspired, and depleted. I kept thinking, "If this is what I'm meant to do, it shouldn't be this hard!" Once again, I realized that something needed to change.

I took a few months to reset my energy and get clear on how I wanted to move forward. As I observed other women I admired in my industry, I realized exactly what I was missing. I'd been so focused on growing my business that I'd completely neglected my Feminine essence. I was stuck in my head and felt disconnected from my heart, my body, and my Soul.

This is when I discovered a beautiful body of work called Feminine Embodiment. I pursued a ten-month certification to learn about embodiment and to become a teacher of this work. During this time, I dove deep into the world of sensuality, movement, and self-expression. In this embodiment exploration process, I became a more authentic, alive, and activated version of myself, which completely transformed the way I was showing up in my life and my business.

While my Soul Calling journey has not been an easy path and has had many twists and turns along the way, every challenge I've experienced has contributed to me finding, expressing, and embodying my purpose. I can truly say that there's nothing more fulfilling and rewarding than knowing that I'm following my passion, creating a positive impact in the world—all while having time-freedom and financial abundance to take care of my own health. What brings me even more joy is witnessing the ripple effect that this work has on my clients' relationships, their families, and their communities. I've seen time and time again that, through living my purpose, other women feel empowered to follow their passions and to pursue their own Soul Callings.

This chapter is designed to inspire and empower you to courageously step into your Soul Calling, and share the highest and most authentic expression of your gifts with the world.

Finding Your Light

I believe that we're all here for a reason. In other words, I believe that your Soul chose to incarnate in this lifetime to make a positive impact. If you've been feeling the call to explore your purpose, do work that feels meaningful, and make a positive impact in the world, you're not alone. This calling you're feeling is right on track with where we are, collectively, in the evolution of spiritual consciousness. Many Souls are being called forward at this time in history to share their unique Soul gifts and support the massive amount of healing that's required for humanity, society, and the earth to come back into harmony.

The first step on the path to discovering your purpose is to connect with what brings you joy and what lights you up the most. When you connect with your own light, you'll gain clarity on the next steps to discover your Soul's Calling—

and, simultaneously, increase your capacity to be of service to others. If you're devoted to sharing your inner light to create a positive impact in the world, you may resonate with the idea of being a Lightworker. In her "Work Your Light" Oracle deck, Rebecca Campbell explains that Lightworkers have a double mission.[11] First, they're here to grow and heal themselves, and second, they're here to contribute their unique Soul gifts to the collective. This is why, as you contribute your Soul gifts to support others in their lives, it lends to greater personal fulfillment, joy, and inspiration.

You may already have noticed a major collective and societal shift when it comes to choosing a vocation and/or career path. We're seeing more and more people following "unconventional" paths and pursuing their passions as healers, coaches, authors, artists, and creatives, rather than choosing more "traditional" professions like medicine, law, business, or working for a large corporation. For some people, following their Soul Calling looks like quitting their corporate careers, starting their own businesses, and becoming a healer, coach, or guide for others. However, just because you wish to make a positive impact in the world doesn't mean your Soul Calling needs to be expressed in any of these specific ways. Your Soul Calling is unique to your Soul. Perhaps your calling is to be an amazing mother, artist, nurse, or teacher. Or maybe you feel happy within your current career path, but you feel called to volunteer your time outside of work to a nonprofit organization that supports animals, children, homelessness, or addiction recovery. The most important thing is that you're actively listening to the guidance of your Soul, prioritizing your own well-being, and, from a place of nourishment and overflow, contributing to the world in a positive way.

I believe that, as we shift into the new paradigm of living in alignment with a greater purpose, it's vitally important to approach this path through The Feminine Way. Rather than carrying over the hyper-Masculine and Ego-focused approach in which we've been operating, we can embrace the Feminine approach by staying connected to our hearts, bodies, and Souls. As we gain clarity and direction, we can follow our purpose in a sustainable way.

Unfortunately, I've seen far too many women, including myself, attempt to follow their purpose from a place of hustle, seeking external validation, and striving to reach their next income goal without honoring their Feminine energy in the process. Inevitably, this imbalanced Masculine approach ends up leading to burnout, a lack of fulfillment, and a toxic cycle of feeling like we're never doing enough. The worst feeling in the world is creating your deepest desire ... only to be too busy and exhausted to enjoy it.

So, what does it look like to infuse The Feminine Way into your journey of following your Soul Calling?

It looks like:

- Creating space each day before work for your daily devotional practices.
- Using your intuition to make aligned decisions.

- Leading from your heart and focusing on being of service.
- Infusing pleasure into your work and allowing yourself to have fun.
- Giving yourself permission to rest and unplug when your body and mind call for it.
- Aligning your work schedule with your menstrual cycle.
- Honoring and alchemizing your emotions as they arise.
- Continuing to focus on other areas of your life outside of work that bring you joy.
- Unapologetically being yourself and letting yourself be seen.

By infusing Feminine principles into your Soul Calling journey, you'll set yourself up for sustainable success and to enjoy the process of bringing your Soul mission to life.

I want to reiterate that this new approach isn't about ignoring the value of Masculine principles of focus, direction, action, and vision. In the same way that it's unhealthy and unsustainable to operate purely from a hyper-Masculine approach, operating only from the Feminine will leave you feeling lost, overwhelmed, and unproductive. It takes practice, but you can blend your inner Masculine and Feminine energies in a harmonious way to create an integrated and balanced approach.

In this chapter, we'll use Feminine principles to explore the different phases of stepping into your Soul Calling and discover how to open yourself to receive abundance through sharing your gifts with the world.

Phase 1: Explore Your Purpose

Discovering your purpose is a spiritual process. Rather than looking externally at various career paths or seeking advice from a career counselor, it's about creating space to listen to your Soul, tuning into your intuition, exploring your natural gifts, and following what lights you up the most.

Follow What Lights You Up

When we're operating in the old paradigm, it's all too common for us to make decisions built on fear-based conditioning rather than heart-based truth. Perhaps you've made decisions based on what you "should" do in an attempt to appease others, or because you're afraid that following your intuition won't work out for you.

The new paradigm is about allowing your Soul to guide you to what feels most true for you. Your Soul didn't come here to work a stressful and unfulfilling job. It wants you to pursue what you're passionate about and to devote your energy to work that lights you up, gives you energy, and makes you feel alive.

The first step to discovering your purpose is to tune in to what you feel most passionate and energized by. The way to do this is to pay attention to what lights you up and brings you joy. You'll know if something is joyful for you because it will feel exciting, expansive, and energizing. For some, this might be painting, dancing, singing, or playing an instrument. For others, it might be cooking, doing physical activity, or going on nature adventures. For others still, bringing people together in community, having authentic conversations with friends, traveling around the world, or teaching workshops on your areas of expertise.

By following what lights you up, you can get into a flow state, which according to Positive Psychology is a "positive mental state of being completely absorbed, focused, and involved in your activities at a certain point in time, as well as deriving enjoyment from being engaged in that activity."[12] When you're in this state, it puts you in an elevated frequency that allows for new creative ideas and opportunities to come through. Rather than trying so hard to figure out the answers for your next steps, focusing on what lights you up and doing more of that will allow answers to come to you with ease.

Exploring What Lights You Up

The following questions can help you to get curious and connect with what lights your Soul on fire. Take some time to journal and reflect on these questions:

1. Looking back on your childhood, what did you do for fun? What were the activities that brought you the most joy?

2. What hobbies or activities are you most drawn to as an adult?
3. What do you enjoy reading or learning about the most?
4. What experiences or activities give you the most energy, inspiration, and excitement?

Once you have a clear list of activities, hobbies, and experiences that light you up, now is the time to start doing one of these activities each week. As you're exploring these activities, pay attention to what opportunities, people, signs, ideas, and synchronicities appear. You can think of this exercise as "following the breadcrumbs" or finding the clues that will guide you toward understanding your purpose.

Soul Curriculum

Another way to gain clarity and insight around your Soul Calling is to reflect on your Soul Curriculum. When your Soul chose to come to this planet, it had certain lessons that it needed to learn as part of your evolution and growth process. Every challenge you've experienced in your life is a lesson that your Soul needed to learn as part of your Soul Curriculum. Each of these lessons has offered you wisdom and insight that you couldn't have learned from any book, podcast, or teacher. Essentially, you had to go through these experiences to learn the lessons and receive the golden nuggets of wisdom for your greatest healing and evolution.

Once you've received the wisdom from your lived experiences, you now have the ability (and responsibility) to share this insight and offer support for others who are experiencing similar challenges. In my case, my challenges with my health, negative body image, sexual shame, going through my divorce, and hitting burnout in my business (just to name a few) have all provided valuable wisdom that I'm now able to use to support and empower others on their journeys.

Soul Curriculum Timeline Exercise

Draw a horizontal line across a piece of paper to represent your Soul Curriculum timeline. Above this line, mark down the significant events, challenges, and/or breakthroughs that you've experienced throughout your life. Underneath the timeline, write down the lessons or "golden nuggets" that you've learned through these events and experiences.

Once you've identified the key lessons you've learned through your Soul Curriculum, you can clearly see the challenges you've had to overcome to get to where you are today. These experiences likely inspired you to become passionate about learning different philosophies and modalities, changing your behaviors, creating better boundaries—and now, leaning more into your Feminine energy and power. All of these factors have equipped you with unique tools to support yourself and others.

There are many people who could benefit from your learned experience of how you made it through your own challenges. You can think about this as "turning your mess into your message." For example, if you've overcome health challenges, left a toxic relationship, or healed from sexual trauma, there are people still in these situations who could benefit from your support to break through and move forward in their lives.

In some cases, you may be ready to start serving others right away. In others, you may need to pursue further education to become qualified (or certified) to safely and effectively guide others. Particularly when it comes to trauma, mental health, medical issues, or financial advice, your own personal healing journey may not be enough to equip you to support others. However, your experience will give you a vital perspective into these issues that others in the field may not possess.

Natural Gifts

Every person has unique gifts and talents to offer to the world—also known as your Soul gifts. Some people are naturally creative, others are naturally intellectual, and others are naturally good at connecting with people. We can discover our unique gifts using various personality profiles such as the Strengths Finder, Enneagram, or Myers-Briggs, and spiritual tools such as Astrology, Human Design, or Gene Keys.

Once you're aware of your natural gifts and skill sets, you can improve upon and expand them with practice. You may feel like your gifts are not unique because there are many other professionals, coaches, leaders, healers, or artists who have gifts similar to your own. However, the truth is that you're a unique being, and your Soul has unique gifts to offer to the world. There's no one else who can express their gifts in the exact same way that you do.

Your natural gifts can also be referred to as your unique Soul Medicine. Your Soul Medicine is something that only you can offer the world. There are plenty of people out there who will resonate with the way you express your gifts. In other words, the people who are meant to find you will find you and resonate with what you have to share.

Some examples of natural gifts include:

- Good listener
- Articulate/good communicator
- Teacher
- Writer
- Creative
- Artistic
- Funny/good sense of humor
- Leadership
- Empathetic
- Organized
- Ambitious
- Analytical
- Tech-savvy

- Problem solver
- Intuitive/psychic

In addition to your natural gifts, it can be helpful to reflect on some of the skill sets you've learned from your current or previous career paths or hobbies that could potentially support or enhance your Soul Calling.

The Unfolding Journey

Once you've completed these three explorations, it's time to see where your passions, Soul Curriculum, and natural gifts intersect. This work will help you get clear on some avenues to explore with regard to your purpose. This is a great time to take out your journal and use your creativity to see how these elements can be weaved together to bring your Soul Calling to life.

Remember that your purpose is unique to you. It doesn't have to fit into a specific career category, and it definitely doesn't have to look like anyone else's purpose. Even if it does look similar to someone else's, the way that you express your purpose is going to be different based on your unique combination of passions, life experiences, and natural gifts. Ultimately, what we're exploring here is how your Soul wants to contribute to the world and be in service to others in a way that feels nourishing and energizing to you as well.

As you can see, there are many different pathways to discover your purpose. I want to remind you that this exploration doesn't have to happen overnight. Discovering your Soul

Calling is an ever-unfolding journey; it's not a destination that you're required to arrive at by a specific age or on a specific timeline, and it's never too late to awaken to your Soul Calling. While you're in the exploration of discovering your purpose, I invite you to bring in the energies of curiosity and patience. There's no need to put pressure on yourself to figure this out all at once.

It's also possible that you still need to go through certain life experiences or discover new aspects of yourself before you can clearly identify your purpose. It may sound cliché, but try to enjoy the journey as much as possible. The more you can release the pressure and allow your purpose to unfold naturally, the faster you'll come to a place of clarity. And remember, even after you get clarity, the ways in which you express your purpose will continue to evolve over time as you yourself evolve.

Jennie's Soul Calling Journey

"I don't understand why I can't get over him. It's been six months since we broke up, but I can't stop thinking about him and wondering if we're going to get back together. I feel so embarrassed that I'm still obsessing over him, and that it's taking up so much of my energy."

As Jennie poured her heart out and shared about the emotional pain she was experiencing, it became clear to both of us that there was a deeper layer of relational healing from her childhood that needed to be addressed. Over the next few months, we explored her relationship dynamics with her parents and previous romantic partnerships. We went into some deep inner child healing and reparenting work.

Week by week, Jennie cultivated a more loving relationship with herself. In doing so, she released her old patterns of codependency and anxious attachment. As Jennie started to see the benefits of relational healing for herself, she became passionate about supporting other women on their self-love and relationship journey.

When we first connected, Jennie was working in a sales job and had a part-time nursing job on the side. The work environment for her sales job was highly toxic, and while she'd always enjoyed helping others, she didn't want to go back to nursing full-time. As our work unfolded, we began to explore her Soul Calling. Jennie signed up for a Nurse Coaching Certification which spoke directly to her passions and her previous work experience as a nurse. While getting her certification, we continued working together to develop her confidence to fully embody her identity as a coach and start sharing her story. As she started to express her gifts publicly, Jennie worked through deeper layers of her own healing, including her fear-based patterns of imposter syndrome, perfectionism, and fear of judgment. At this point, she tapped into her natural gifts for writing and speaking to empower other women.

Within a few months of showing up consistently in her unique truth and Soul Calling, Jennie onboarded her first coaching client to support them on their self-love and relationship healing journey. Within her coaching model, she got to use her superpowers (aka natural gifts) of empathy, intuition, and leadership to guide her clients through their own transformation journey.

When I asked Jennie what her favorite part about coaching was, she said, "Seeing my clients progress as they heal toxic relationship patterns brings me so much joy. There are no words to describe how rewarding it feels to know that I'm living my purpose and making a positive impact in the world. I have a deep sense of fulfillment, and my heart feels like it's bursting with love and positive energy. I know that this is exactly what my Soul came here to do."

Phase 2: Embody Your Purpose

Once you've identified your purpose (or at least identified a small aspect of it), there's a whole next level of growth required to actually start sharing your gifts and creating a positive impact in the world around you. It's one thing to know what your purpose is, but it's a whole different story to put yourself out there and step into a new identity as a leader, coach, healer, teacher, speaker, artist, musician, or whatever it is you're feeling called to do.

Even though your Soul knows you came here for this reason, your Ego will do whatever it takes to stop you from stepping out of your comfort zone. Remember, your Ego is terrified of the unknown. Similar to what I shared about the beginning of my own Soul Calling journey: when you take action toward stepping into your calling, your Ego will bring up all of your fears, doubts, and insecurities so that you don't risk failing or being judged by others. When these fears are present, you might struggle with procrastination, inaction, or self-sabotage, as well as a sense of inner turmoil because your Soul is guiding you forward but your Ego is blocking you from taking action. For this reason, many Lightworkers will suppress their Soul Calling, or push it aside until they feel "ready" or have a specific plan for success. However, if you don't learn how to overcome your fears, then frustration, overwhelm, and depression can arise. If you're in this place, the most important thing you can do is learn how to identify, acknowledge, and dance with your fears so that you can get out of your own way. Needless to say, it takes a tremendous amount of courage, resilience, and perseverance to follow your Soul Calling and embody your identity as a Feminine leader.

Here's a five-step process to learn how to dance with your fears.

Step 1: Identify

Become aware of the fears that are present in your mind as you start to take action toward your purpose. These Ego-based fears are often rooted in the wounded Masculine way of thinking about success, productivity, and wealth. When these fears are present, take note that they're not coming from your authentic truth; they're coming from your logical mind.

Some of the most common fears that may arise as you venture down this path are:

- ***Imposter syndrome:*** Feeling like you have no idea what you're doing, and like you're a fraud. In your mind, this could sound like: "Who am I to do this?" or "What if they find out that I'm not really who I say I am?"
- ***Fear of judgment:*** Fear of other people judging you for being too weird, too much, too loud, too spiritual, or too selfish. This could sound like: "What if they think I'm crazy?" "What if they think I'm ugly?" or "What if they think I'm stupid?"
- ***Fear of failure:*** Worrying that you won't be successful and that you'll disappoint yourself or others. This could sound like: "What if I fail?" "What if 'they' were right?" or "What if this doesn't work out?"
- ***Unworthiness:*** Feeling like you don't have enough value to offer, or like you don't deserve to be successful. This could sound like: "I'm not good enough," "Who would actually pay me for this?" or "What value do I even have to offer?"
- ***Scarcity:*** Fear that there's not enough time, money, or resources to do what you're called to do, or that

resources are going to run out. This could sound like: "What if I can't support myself financially?" or "There are already too many people doing what I want to do; there won't be clients left for me."

Step 2: Acknowledge

Once you've identified the fears, the next step is to acknowledge them without judgment. It can be easy to feel like there's something wrong with you, but instead of going down the shame spiral, the invitation is to get curious about the fears that are coming up, and recognize that these fears are just your Ego trying to keep you safe.

Step 3: Release

If you feel frustrated, sad, hopeless, disappointed, or anxious, give yourself space to feel these emotions. When you allow yourself to release the emotions and the fears associated with them, you'll reclaim your power and come back into alignment with your truth more quickly. You can use the Emotional Alchemy process from Chapter Five to move through your feelings. As a refresher, some other ways to process your emotions in a healthy way include breathwork, journaling, talking to a friend or therapist, dancing, screaming, shaking, or crying.

Step 4: Upgrade

This is where you intentionally shift back into your Feminine power and realign with your faith in the Universe. One way to do this is through an affirmation practice where you say affirmations out loud to yourself in the mirror or write them down in your journal. Alternatively, you can listen to an uplifting podcast, inspiring song, guided meditation, or read a few pages of an empowering book to bring you back to a state of faith and confidence.

Step 5: Action

Come back to your devotional practices to create space to listen to your intuitive guidance. Ask your inner knowing, "What is one baby step I can take towards my Soul Calling?"

Once you're clear on what to do next, there's no more room for hesitation. This is the time to take clear, courageous action. Your mind might tell you that you need to know the whole plan before you move forward, but that's not how it works. When you take baby steps toward your passions and your dreams, new opportunities, connections, and possibilities will open up for you that you didn't even know existed. It's as if the Universe is rewarding you for courageously leaning into the unknown and following your truth.

While it's important to be consistent in taking aligned action toward your Soul Calling, it's equally as important to honor the dance between "doing" and "being"—between taking action and stepping back for rest and nourishment. Remember, this is your life's work, not a twelve-month game plan. When you finish a big project or take a brave leap, it's okay to take some time to celebrate, rest, and recalibrate before you rush into the next thing. Taking breaks and honoring your rest time is just as essential for your long-term success as daily productivity.

Phase 3: Express Yourself

Stepping into your Soul Calling is one of the most vulnerable and courageous things you can do. It's a re-identification process where you're becoming a new version of yourself and allowing yourself to be seen as the Lightworker, healer, coach, artist, and/or creative that you are. Up until this point in your life, you may have suppressed your thoughts, questions, and beliefs because you were afraid of making people uncomfortable, or afraid they would judge you. In the expression phase of stepping into your Soul Calling, there's no more room for hiding or playing small. This is your time to shine your light and let yourself be seen and heard.

As you do this, you'll likely revisit all of your fears of judgment and imposter syndrome that we spoke about earlier. This is natural and to be expected. Remember, these fears are a survival mechanism tied to your Ego. To some extent, putting yourself out there does put you at higher risk for judgment and rejection—but in our modern society, rejection doesn't equal death. In fact, it can lead to liberation. So, when these fears come up, come back to the Feminine principles you've learned in this book, and work through them using the devotion, intuition, pleasure, and Emotional Alchemy practices.

When you step into your new identity, the reality is that not everyone is going to like what you have to share. Some people will feel triggered or intimidated by your fullest expression. Some people who've been in your life for a long time may no longer be an energetic match with the person you're becoming. It's very likely that you'll go through a process of releasing friendships that are no longer in alignment. This can seem really scary while it's happening, but don't worry too much. Before you know it, you'll start attracting like-minded people into your life who are a better match for who you're becoming. These are the people who are going to embrace your authentic expression and inspire you to be even more of who you are.

When it comes to putting yourself out there, it's important you choose the forms of expression that feel most authentic to you. Instead of just following the latest trend or trying to copy what other successful people are doing, try to connect with your own creative expression.

Some forms of creative expression you can play with are:

- Writing
- Speaking
- Dancing

- Singing
- Acting
- Fashion
- Design
- Painting
- Comedy
- Spoken word
- Photography (or being photographed)

Your unique authentic expression will always magnetize the right opportunities and clients your way.

As you continue to explore, express, and embody your Soul Calling, you'll discover that this process is simply an extension of your Feminine journey. Living in your purpose is living in the highest alignment with your heart and Soul. It's the way you contribute your love, your beauty, and your essence to the collective. As you express your Soul Calling in the world, not only will you create a positive impact but you will also be an example of what's possible for others who desire to live a life of freedom, purpose, and abundance. By living in your purpose, you'll create a ripple effect that extends far beyond what your mind can comprehend.

Opening to Receive Abundance

One final yet essential piece to successfully stepping into your Soul Calling is aligning with abundance consciousness—most importantly, opening to receive abundance.

Most of us grew up with fear-based scarcity consciousness. If you come from an upbringing where security was more important than happiness, it can feel terrifying to think about pursuing your passions without having a steady paycheck every two weeks. Growing up, you may have received messages like, "Money doesn't grow on trees," or "You need to have a stable and secure job or you'll end up on the street," or "The only way to make more money is to work harder." Disempowering stories like these are the reason why many people are too afraid to follow their dreams. And while it's true that going down the path of Soulpreneurship is more risky and less predictable than having a stable nine-to-five job, it's absolutely possible to be successful while doing work that you love and are passionate about.

While scarcity consciousness teaches us that there's never enough, abundance consciousness teaches us that we live in an abundant Universe, and that there are infinite resources available to us. When we're operating from scarcity consciousness, we come from a place of fear and lack which can lead to inaction, self-sabotage, and procrastination. Scarcity will tell you that any uncertainty is a threat to your survival, particularly when it comes to money. Alternatively, when you are operating from a place of Feminine abundance and faith, you'll take the actions necessary to move forward with your goals, even if those actions don't make logical sense. You'll take risks when they're supported by your intuitive guidance, and do what's required to attract all the clients, opportunities, and money that are available to you. When you're aligned with The Feminine Way and open to receiving abundance, there's a sense of receptivity—of allowing abundance to flow to you with ease, rather than striving, struggling, and forcing your way to success.

The concept of "receiving" can feel extra challenging for women because we often take on the role of givers, nurturers, and caretakers. In many ways, we've not learned or mastered the Feminine art of receiving. One of the ways you can open to receive more abundance is to practice receiving in other areas of your life. This could look like accepting support when other people offer to help with something, graciously receiving compliments instead of deflecting them, or having a willingness to ask for and receiving more love and affection from your romantic partner, friends, or family.

To truly understand how abundance works in The Feminine Way, you can think about money as energy. When you're open and receptive, you become like a clear riverbed, allowing money to flow to you with ease. When you're in fear and lack, you create resistance or "dams" in your energetic field, and therefore block money from flowing to you or divert it around you. If you've struggled with money in the past or have never had an abundance of money in your bank account, it can be helpful to zoom out and acknowledge the abundance that you have in other areas of your life. For example, look around and see the abundance of water, air, and nature that's available to you right now. Or you can tap into the abundance of support, love, and connection that you have access to.

All in all, your Soul Calling requires a combination of Feminine attraction and magnetism along with Masculine action and focus. As we established in the beginning of this book, a healthy balance that supports your unique energy and personality is the ultimate goal of The Feminine Way. By incorporating the Feminine wisdom of abundance and receiving, you'll undoubtedly reach your goals with more ease, while at the same time experiencing more enjoyment and pleasure along the way.

The process of aligning with abundance is exactly the same as the process of "dancing with your fears" that we covered earlier in this chapter. It starts with identifying that scarcity is present, acknowledging the feeling or thought without judgment, releasing the energy of scarcity through feeling the emotion and/or moving it through your body, upgrading your thoughts to realign with the energy of abundance, and taking inspired action toward your vision. If you still find yourself feeling stuck in a scarcity mindset, bring your thoughts to a place of gratitude for all of the abundance you currently have in your life and remind yourself of the evidence that you're safe and supported in this moment.

Taking the Leap

Going all in on your Soul Calling is one of the biggest acts of surrender and trust that you'll choose in your lifetime. That said, each person's version of "going all in" is different. For some, taking this leap might look like intentionally saving money until they have an emergency fund or safety net to feel ready to start their own business. For others, it may look like pitching to investors or applying for a business loan. For others it might look like keeping a part-time job for a while as they set the foundation for their business. For still others, it might look like accumulating the skill sets to change to a new job in an industry or with a company they resonate with deeply. No matter which path you choose, however, there will come a point when you'll have to make the courageous choice of letting go of your backup plan to go all in on your vision. The amount of time it takes to get to a place of "readiness" is not important. What matters most is that you're listening to your Soul and your intuition, not your head, and taking baby steps toward your vision every day despite any fears that emerge. Soon, you'll be actively contributing your wisdom and your gifts to the world in a way that feels energizing and fulfilling.

Freedom-Based Living

Following your truth, living in alignment with your Soul Calling, and receiving abundance in exchange for your gifts lends itself to the freedom-based lifestyle that so many

Feminine beings yearn for. Rather than feeling stuck and depleted in a career or life path that drains your life force energy and limits your ability to enjoy your life, this new paradigm offers the opportunity to create your life by design. In having more time-freedom and more energy from doing work that lights your Soul on fire, it allows you to honor your Feminine needs for nourishment, connection, and pleasure. It also creates more space and flexibility to honor your cyclical nature as a Feminine being.

In the next chapter, we'll explore how to align your life with your feminine rhythms and cycles to create more harmony within your career path, your health, and your relationships.

Soul Reflections

- If you could do anything with your time and energy—and you weren't worried about money or what other people thought about your decisions—what would you spend your time doing?
- In what ways do you feel called to express your creativity? Remember, you don't have to be amazing at your creative expression to begin with; simply focus on what feels the most inspiring and interesting to you!
- Imagine yourself five years from now living fully in alignment with your purpose. What would your life look and feel like?

- What is one baby step you can take today toward the vision you just described?
- What is your relationship with the concept of receiving? Do you feel open to receive abundance, support, and love from others? If not, what are some ways you can start practicing receiving in your life right now?

"We often forget that we are nature. Nature is not something separate from us. So when we say that we have lost our connection to nature, we've lost our connection to ourselves."

Andy Goldsworthy

chapter eight

Cyclical Living

I sat alone in my home office, blankly staring at my computer screen. I'd just completed the biggest launch of my career, and I was exhausted. I had everything I could possibly want in my business, but something still felt off.

As the familiar feeling of anxiety and overwhelm took over my body, I closed my computer, walked out of my office, and sat on the couch next to my boyfriend. I looked him in the eyes and said, "Babe, I'm so tired right now. I feel like I should be more excited about reaching this amazing milestone, but I don't feel like this is sustainable. I can't keep working like this. I didn't start my business to just make money and work all the time. I want to feel more alive. I want to have more fun. I want to enjoy my work again. Something has to change."

There were many red flag moments leading up to this point of burnout. My intuition had been telling me that something was off in my business for a while, but I didn't listen because I didn't feel like pausing was an option. I was afraid that if I didn't keep producing at such a high level, all of my success would go away and I wouldn't be able to support myself. At the time, I couldn't see a different way of doing things; all of the successful mentors and coaches I looked up to were using the same strategies, so in my mind, this was the only pathway to success. But while my bank account looked great and my career was heading in the right direction on paper, my Soul was clearly telling me to figure out a different way.

Once again, I was at a crossroads: I could either keep pushing forward with my Masculine energy, or I could surrender and open myself up to the Feminine wisdom that was begging for me to listen. The thought of slowing down and trying a different approach felt terrifying. At times, it literally felt like I was dying, and that my business wasn't going to survive. I know this sounds dramatic, but my Ego was *really* unhappy with the idea of me taking my foot off the gas. It felt like, after all the hard work I'd put into my business, I was going backward—but, at the same time, there was a deeper part of me that knew everything would somehow be okay.

Looking back, I can see that I'd been burning the candle at both ends and completely ignoring my cyclical nature. Even though I was doing my daily devotion practices and taking good care of my body, I was still spending way too much time in front of my computer and pushing my business forward using my Masculine energy. In my case, "burnout" wasn't a rapid collapse but a gradual progression getting incrementally worse each day.

Once I recognized that my own patterns of constant "doing" weren't sustainable, I realized I needed to look at my unconscious beliefs around success. It was time to unlearn and dismantle the programming around scarcity and unworthiness that had been driving me forward in an unhealthy and unsustainable way.

Over the next six months, I downsized my team, took a break from launching new programs, and focused on my inner healing. As I started this uncomfortable journey of slowing down, my Ego had a daily freak-out where it would tell me I was "lazy" and that I would "never be successful again." These beliefs triggered my nervous system into fight-or-flight mode, and I would either find myself hysterically crying or obsessively strategizing about how to grow my business. Each time this pattern happened, I took a deep breath and used my embodiment practices to bring my nervous system back to a calm state. I also hired a business mindset coach who specialized in burnout, and worked with a therapist to help me move through this challenging transition.

Miraculously, as I was doing this deep inner work, several previous clients reached out to ask if I had any spots open for private coaching. My podcast audience also continued to grow without any additional effort. I kept receiving little signs from the Universe that I was on the right track, and that everything was going to be okay. After a few months, my fears got quieter, and I allowed myself to keep surrendering to the process.

I envisioned a business that felt easeful, intuitive, fun, and enjoyable. I focused on the parts of my business that felt light and inspiring, and started to release all of the projects and tasks that felt like they were weighing me down. I created more space for resting, spending time with friends, and enjoying my life than I ever had before.

Within a few months, I noticed that I was waking up with more energy. Creative ideas were flowing to me without any effort. I started to feel excited about my business again, and felt a rush of inspiration to create a new offering for my community. This time, it didn't come from a place of following a fancy strategy or figuring out the perfect messaging; instead, it felt like I was being pulled forward to create a program that came from my Soul. Once I completed the outline for the program, I shared it with my community and ended up having my first successful *and* easeful launch.

For the rest of the year, I continued to let my Feminine guide the way. Before I knew it, my business income had exceeded the amount I made the year before, except this time I worked far fewer hours and enjoyed the process a lot more.

While my burnout and Feminine business journey is unique to my own path, burnout can and does happen to many women at some point in their lives. For many of the women I work with, burnout sneaks up on them so slowly that they don't even realize it's happening until they hit a wall. Instead of listening to their Soul's cues, they keep going until their body stops them—until they get too sick to get out of bed or have a mental health breakdown. Moreover, burnout doesn't only happen in business. It can come from motherhood, caretaking an elderly parent, or any other prolonged or acute period of stress.

Regardless of the journey that brought you to this place, learning how to honor your cyclical nature is the pathway to recovering your vitality. In this chapter, we'll explore what it means to honor your cyclical nature and how to use sacred rituals to prevent burnout from reoccurring.

Mother Nature is Our Guide

The concepts of slowing down, replenishing, and listening to our body's needs are highly undervalued and have been viewed as inconvenient or unproductive in our Western culture. We receive constant messages from society such as, "Work hard, play hard," "You can rest when you're dead," "Don't be so lazy" or "Push through the pain." Through these messages, we've learned to ignore the wisdom of our bodies and to disregard our fundamental need for rest and recovery.

Many people walk around wearing their busyness and stress as a badge of honor, but in fact it's an addiction: staying busy helps them stave off feelings of unworthiness, pain, and scarcity. This hyper-productive approach may work for a short time, but eventually it becomes unsustainable. Our continual dismissal of our cyclical nature has led to increasing rates of burnout, depression, anxiety, hormonal imbalances, and stress-related physical health conditions. And as we've become increasingly disconnected from our personal rhythms and cycles, so too have we become disconnected from nature.

Nature is never linear. It operates on a cyclical rhythm. It moves in seasons, rhythms, ebbs and flows. So too does the Feminine. We can look to Mother Nature as our greatest teacher of how to realign with our own cyclical nature.

Throughout the year, nature progresses through different seasons: spring, summer, fall, and winter. Each season is part of the natural life cycle of the earth and takes place exactly when and where it needs to so the earth and every living thing can thrive. These deep and natural rhythms exist in perfect order; if winter and fall didn't exist, and trees would be forced to produce fruit all year long, the soil would become depleted and the fruit wouldn't be as flavorful or nutritious. Eventually, the trees would sicken and decay. Conversely, if spring and summer didn't exist, the fruit couldn't grow without the energy from the sun. In every aspect of Mother Nature, we see evidence that honoring the seasons is the best way to sustain our vitality and growth.

The same goes for your own body. Your hormones and nervous system weren't designed to be in fight-or-flight mode for long periods of time. Your body needs periods of rest and recovery in order to support your physical and emotional well-being. What if, instead of resisting your own "seasons," you decided to accept or even embrace them?

The Feminine is here to remind you that when you honor your natural rhythms and cycles, you release resistance to your true nature. You've been taught to operate as a linear being, when in fact you're a cyclical being. You're not a robot or a machine designed to operate at full capacity 24/7; you're a living being that's meant to experience the ebb and flow of life in all its complexity and beauty.

Coming back into alignment with your cyclical nature is not so much a process of learning something new, but a process of remembrance and Soul recognition. When you embrace your natural cycles, you'll no longer wait until you reach the point of exhaustion to listen to your body. Instead, you'll become more attuned with your own rhythms and learn how to honor what your body needs on a daily basis. This practice will help you to reduce the frequency of stress, overwhelm, and exhaustion you're experiencing, and support you in feeling more energy, vibrancy, and flow in all facets of your life.

In this next section, we'll explore a variety of different cycles, including your daily, weekly, monthly, and seasonal cycles, to help you reconnect to your cyclical nature.

Honoring Your Daily Cycle

Your body has a biological circadian rhythm, a twenty-four-hour cycle that's governed by your sleep and wake cycles. Your cortisol (stress hormone) is naturally supposed to rise in the morning when the sun comes out, giving you more energy and drive, and decrease in the evening when it gets dark out, prompting rest and relaxation.

Before we had electricity and technology, it was much easier to honor this natural rhythm. However, now that we have artificial lighting and unlimited access to electronic devices, it's become increasingly more challenging to maintain a healthy circadian rhythm.

In addition to these external biological effects that have happened over time, it's become "normal" in our Western culture to consume excessive amounts of caffeine and, for many, to work late into the evening, which throws off our natural hormonal cycles even more.

Being out of balance with your circadian rhythm for long periods of time can lead to all kinds of physical and emotional symptoms including anxiety, difficulty with mental clarity and focus, fatigue, weight gain, difficulty losing weight, and auto-immune conditions. Coming back into balance with your natural circadian rhythm will not only help you to feel more energized throughout the day, but it will also help to stabilize your blood sugar and metabolism.

Here are some steps you can take to get back on track with your circadian rhythm:

- Create a consistent and healthy sleep schedule.
- Get outside in the morning to absorb natural sunlight.
- Reduce your caffeine intake and/or have a cut-off time so that it doesn't keep you up late.
- Reduce exposure to screens in the evening and/or use blue light blocking glasses or filters.

Sleep Cycle Exercise

The first step to coming back into alignment with your circadian rhythm is to bring awareness to your current sleep cycle. For one week, write down what time you go to sleep and what time you wake up. Once you start to notice the patterns of your sleep cycles, it can help you to start being more intentional about what time you go to sleep. You may wish to use a device like the Oura Ring or an app on your phone to track your sleep patterns.

If you have trouble falling asleep, I've found with my clients that it's helpful to have an intentional wind-down period at the end of the day to help reduce their cortisol levels before they go to sleep. This might look like setting a notification on your calendar that reminds you to turn off your electronics and start preparing your body for rest. During this time, you can drink some non-caffeinated tea, take a warm bath, listen to a guided meditation, read a book, or do some light stretching.

I recommend taking an incremental approach to this process where you start by going to sleep thirty minutes earlier than you currently are, and gradually work your way to going to sleep at a healthy time for you. If you're a parent with young children and you have an unpredictable sleep schedule, do your best to honor your sleep hygiene by getting into bed earlier. If you have support from a spouse or caregiver, work out a clear schedule so you can get adequate rest. If you're a shift worker and aren't able to align your sleep schedule with the natural transitions of day into night, do your best to create a consistent routine for yourself and honor your energy levels during your waking hours so that you don't add additional stress to your system with intense physical activity.

Daily Nature Medicine

In our technology-focused society, it's easy to get stuck inside all day staring at your phone or your computer screen. This way of operating will keep you in a hyper-Masculine state unless you consciously choose to break the pattern. Regardless of how busy your day is, spending at least a few minutes in nature can help to reduce your stress levels.

Incorporating more nature time into your life could look like going for a walk around the block, sitting on a bench in the park while you eat lunch, or putting your bare feet directly on the earth, a technique which is also known as "grounding" or "Earthing." According to a 2020 article in *Science Direct*, the practice of Earthing "stabilizes the physiology at the deepest levels, reduces inflammation, pain, and stress, improves blood flow, energy, and sleep, and generates greater well-being."[13]

Nature has a powerful way of calming down your nervous system. I often refer to my time in nature as "nature medicine" because I always notice a significant shift in my emotions and energy whenever I spend time outside. As you deepen your connection with nature, you'll naturally start to feel more connected to your own cyclical nature.

Nature Date Exercise

For the next seven days, put a ten-minute block of time in your calendar for a "nature date." If you have access to some grass or sand, consider an "Earthing" practice where you spend time barefoot or lying on the ground. You can also meditate, focus on your breathing, and/or pay attention to the colors or the sounds that you're experiencing. Whatever activity you choose, I encourage you to leave your phone inside or turn it to airplane mode so that you can be present with this exercise.

After seven days, check in with yourself to see what shifts you've noticed with your stress levels and/or emotional well-being.

Re-Writing Your Weekly Cycle

According to the international calendar, our seven-day week is split up into five workdays and two weekend (or rest) days. With such a long and demanding work week, it can be easy to get into the cycle of "living for the weekend" and ignoring your need for rest or pleasure throughout the rest of the week.

As an entrepreneur, I've explored several different ways to structure my schedule during the week. Figuring out the optimal schedule that allows me to have the best energy and mental clarity has been a process, but what I've found is that it can be helpful to group particular tasks or projects into certain days of the week. For example, on Mondays I try not to schedule any meetings or client sessions so that I can focus on creative projects and administrative tasks. On Fridays, I like to focus on podcast interviewing and wrapping up any final projects from the week. This means that Tuesday through Thursday are the days where I have the most energy output with client calls and meetings.

If you don't work for yourself, your schedule may have less flexibility, however there are ways you can start to be more intentional with your schedule to create more flow between your Masculine and Feminine energy throughout the week. This could look like blocking off your calendar during your lunch break so you can step away from your computer while eating your lunch. Or it could look like scheduling time before and/or after work to do something creative, fun, or nourishing for your body.

It's also important to be intentional with your work boundaries. If you find yourself working longer hours than you're being paid for, or constantly checking your work email on the weekends, it's time to set healthier boundaries so you can make time for your self-care and well-being. At first this may seem challenging, because not only are you used to overworking but it's likely your colleagues and/or your boss are used to you responding during those hours. Because of this, there will naturally be an adjustment period—but eventually, everyone will benefit from you taking good care of yourself.

Designing Your Schedule Exercise

Use a pen and paper to map out your ideal schedule throughout the week. Let yourself get creative and write down what your most nourishing and simultaneously productive week would look like.

After you write down your ideal schedule, take a look at your current schedule and see where you can make some minor adjustments. If possible, make the first set of changes within one week of today.

Honoring Your Monthly Cycle

For many women, the word "cycle" is most closely associated with our menstrual cycle. It's the cycle that most of us know and are intimately familiar with from the first time we start our periods all the way through the season of menopause. So much of our lives as women are impacted by our monthly cycle, yet, despite the fact that this is a natural, normal process, there's an overwhelming amount of shame associated with menstruation. Because of this shame, it's common for women to feel like their periods are dirty or disgusting, which in turn leads them to hide or diminish the symptoms they experience during their monthly menstruation.

Based on what we've already explored about the dangers of ignoring our daily and weekly cycles, I'll bet you can guess what can happen when we ignore or diminish our monthly cycles. Bernadette Dijkhuizen-Keogh, therapist and mindfulness coach, put it well: "A woman's body is an intricate system with constantly shifting moods and energy." We're always shifting, always changing, ebbing and flowing in our own unique natural rhythms, and yet the majority of us pretend like we aren't. Cultural shame, religious stigma, and plain old misogyny have real, harmful consequences.

Let's explore this together further. Think back to your experience when you first got your period. Did you feel educated about your period before you got it? Did you feel any shame or embarrassment? How did other people in your family or community respond when you got your period? If you felt embarrassed about your period when you were younger, it's likely that you've unconsciously disowned other Feminine parts of yourself as well.

Another reason why women become disconnected from their menstrual cycle is because they start taking birth control at a young age, whether as pregnancy prevention or to mask the symptoms that come with hormonal imbalances. When a woman is on birth control, she'll experience less variation throughout the month with her mood, energy and physical symptoms. In some cases, depending on the form of birth control, she may skip her period altogether and not experience the very natural monthly shedding that's supposed to take place. Long-term use of birth control can not only lead women to feel less in tune with their bodies, but some studies show that it can also lead to hormonal imbalances or dysregulation down the road.

Coming back into harmony with your natural cycles starts with coming into a healthy relationship with menstruation. Menstruation is a natural and miraculous cycle that allows for fertility to occur. Without the menstrual cycle, human life wouldn't exist.

In many ancient cultures, the female menstrual cycle was seen as sacred. When women were on their periods, they were said to be more psychic and connected to their intuition. In many cultures throughout the world, including Native American, Chinese, and African, women used to gather together in separate huts, tents, or designated areas to honor this sacred time.

More recently, as global rates of female health issues and hormone imbalances have increased, more women are being called to resurrect these ancient practices and heal their relationship with their menstrual cycles.

The Inner Seasons

The next step in cultivating a deeper relationship with your menstrual cycle is to become more educated on the four distinct phases or "inner seasons" that you experience each month. Namely, these four phases are the menstrual, follicular, ovulation, and luteal.

Honoring your cyclical nature is about listening to your body and paying attention to the different moods and energies that you're experiencing throughout the month.

Day 1 to 5—Menstrual Phase (period)
Inner winter: slow, sensitive, quiet, introspective, inward.

Day 6 to 16–Follicular Phase (pre-ovulation)
Inner spring: focused, creative, action-oriented.

Day 17 to 22–Ovulation Phase (ovulating)
Inner summer: sensual, social, adventurous.

Day 23 to 29–Luteal Phase (winding down)
Inner autumn: learning, ideas, hunger, stillness.[14]

The above information is based on a twenty-nine-day menstrual cycle. If your cycle is naturally longer or if you have an irregular cycle, these windows may vary. The exact days listed in the chart are not as important as connecting with your own body and recognizing the shifts between your inner seasons.

Note: If you've already entered the season of menopause, have had a hysterectomy, or for any other reason do not menstruate, this doesn't mean that you don't have a monthly cycle. The hormonal cycles that triggered menstruation may still be taking place in your body, but on a less intense level. If you don't get regular periods, you can still track your monthly cycles using the tools in the next section. Or you can simply observe your natural flow of emotions, moods, and physical sensations as they correspond to the phases of the moon—just like ancient wise women once did.

Getting in touch with my own menstrual cycle and honoring my body's needs each month has been one of the greatest gifts

I've given to myself and those around me. One of the main ways I've committed to honoring my cycle is by looking ahead at my schedule each month and making sure that I'm not overcommitting to any social events or business tasks during the days leading up to my period and during the first two days of my cycle. I know that, during this specific time period, my mind is not as focused, my emotions are more sensitive, and my body needs more rest. So, I make a point to schedule speaking engagements and social activities during my spring and summer seasons, when I have more creativity and energy. I've also chosen to honor my menstrual cycle by modifying my exercise and nutrition according to how my body is feeling in each season. If my body is asking for rest during my fall or winter seasons, I do lower-intensity exercise and increase my rest time. By aligning my lifestyle and business with my menstrual cycle, I've experienced more ease, flow, and harmony in every facet of my life.

Now it's your turn! The first step is learning how to track your menstrual cycle, and then start getting curious about how you can make choices to align with your own flow.

Menstrual Cycle Tracking Exercise

One of the best ways to get in touch with the different phases in your cycle is to start tracking your menstrual cycle and pay attention to your emotions and physical sensations throughout the month. Keep in mind that your menstrual cycle doesn't just include the days when you have your period, but rather, as mentioned above, a twenty-eight to thirty-one-day (or longer) cycle. If you're new to tracking your cycle, start by downloading a period-tracking app, or learn about the Fertility Awareness method which is a more accurate way of tracking your cycle. Additionally, you can keep a journal next to your bed and write down any changes in your energy, mood, or physical body throughout the month to see if you notice patterns or trends.

Connecting with the Moon Cycles

Paying attention to the lunar cycles is another way to deepen your connection with Mother Nature and your own cyclical nature. In each month of the Zodiac calendar, there's a full moon and a new moon. When you start to connect with the moon cycles, it's likely that certain patterns in your energy correspond to the lunar phases.

Before I started paying attention to the lunar cycles, I didn't realize that the energy of the moon was directly impacting my own energy and my menstrual cycle. Some months, I would notice that around the full moon I was more tired, emotional, and introspective. I also found it fascinating that many women's menstrual cycles (when they're not on birth control) are naturally aligned with either the full moon or the new moon. My menstrual cycle used to start on the full moon, and then at some point it switched to the new moon. I now start my period within days of the new moon every month.

Full Moon and New Moon Rituals

Moon circles are monthly rituals that date back centuries. The full moon and the new moon are the most powerful times for rituals. Moon rituals are a great way to harness the Feminine energy of the moon, and also an opportunity to gather together in community with other women.

A full moon or new moon ceremony can begin with some type of meditation and/or journaling to connect with how you're feeling. Generally speaking, the full moon represents a time of introspection and looking at any "shadows," fears, habits, or limiting beliefs that you're ready to let go of. On the other hand, the new moon represents new beginnings and is a great time to set intentions for the month ahead.

If you're curious to learn more about gathering with women for a moon circle, check with your local yoga studios, spiritual shops, or women's circles. There are also many online gatherings to choose from if you don't find a group in your area.

Aligning with the Seasons

Depending on where you live in the world, you may or may not have four distinct seasons throughout the year. For most of my early life, I lived in Southern California, where there's not much variation in the weather throughout the year. However, when I moved to the mountains of Asheville in North Carolina, I started to feel a significant difference in my energy based on the seasons. For example, during the winter, I found I was much more introspective and had less desire to attend social events, even though I'm naturally an extrovert. As soon as spring came around, I noticed a huge shift in my energy and a desire to be socializing and hosting in-person events again.

One of the easiest ways to reconnect with the rhythms of the seasons, no matter what part of the world you live in, is to incorporate quarterly rituals throughout the year. We can use the "changing of the seasons" to tune into the energy of the season we're entering, and as an opportunity for self-reflection and intention setting for the months ahead. In the Zodiac calendar, the seasonal changes are marked by the summer solstice, winter solstice, spring equinox, and autumn equinox.

Connecting with the Seasons Ritual

Ritual for honoring the changing of the seasons:

1. Create an altar using flowers, crystals, candles, or any other sacred items that feel significant for you. These items can also be representative of the season you're entering at the time of the ritual.
2. Do some research to learn about the significance of the solstice or equinox you're working with.
3. Take out your journal and reflect on the past three months (from the last solstice or the last equinox)

to reflect on how you've grown and/or what you've created in your life.

4. Feel into the next three months ahead and connect to what you would like to manifest and/or what you want to focus on with your personal growth.
5. Make an offering back to nature. This could look like placing flowers or fruit onto the earth and expressing gratitude for all that nature provides for you, or just taking time to be outside and put your hands on a tree.

This ritual can be done on your own, or you can invite friends, your children, or your partner, to perform this ritual together. If you gather with one or more people for this ritual, consider sharing your celebrations and your manifestations out loud, which increases the potency of this ritual.

Customizing Your Cyclical Nature Journey

One of the greatest gifts of slowing down and honoring your cyclical nature is that you'll naturally create space to focus on activities and experiences that bring more pleasure and fulfillment into your life. In case you need a permission slip, this is your reminder that it's okay to slow down, enjoy your life, and intentionally create opportunities to find pleasure. It's okay to take breaks, go on vacation, and to enjoy your life. Everything has its proper season.

We've reviewed many different cycles and practices in this chapter, and I encourage you to work with them all—but you don't need to implement them all at once. If you're new to cyclical living, start by focusing on your daily circadian rhythm. Then, when you feel like you have an energetic capacity, turn your attention to the other cycles. As always, I invite you to use your intuition to see which cycles you feel drawn to work with first.

In the next chapter, we'll explore Feminine Embodiment principles that will help you continue to attune to your body in a more intimate way and show up as your most authentic self in all areas of your life.

Soul Reflections

- Based on the different cycles we covered in this chapter, what are the top two cycles that you feel would be the most valuable for you to focus on (daily, weekly, monthly, or seasonal)?
- How would you describe your current relationship with your menstrual cycle? How can you be more intentional about honoring your monthly cycle? (You can answer these questions regardless of whether you get your period or not.)
- What are some ways you can prioritize more rest or spaciousness into your daily, weekly, monthly, and/or annual schedule? For example: Intentionally

scheduling two vacations per year; choosing to take a social media break once a week; deleting or locking your email app from your phone on the weekend; setting a time limit for screens to transition to a pre-bedtime meditation ritual.

"There is a whole universe of magic living in your body,
as you breathe in each moment filled with wonder
and mystery of the incomprehensible divine."

Tara Teng

chapter nine

Feminine Embodiment

I rushed into the dance studio and took my place at the wooden ballet barre. Standing up tall in front of the floor-to-ceiling mirrors, I saw my torso wrapped tight in a black leotard with sheer pink tights hugging my thighs. Hair pulled back in a perfectly placed bun on top of my head. Classmates chattering and giggling in the background. Anxiety building and tears welling up in my eyes. This audition felt like the most important thing in my world.

A loud voice in my head said, "Why would *you* get the lead role? Your thighs are too big and you aren't as flexible as the other girls in your class. You can't possibly get chosen as the lead dancer."

Sure enough, I didn't get selected for the role. My teacher chose another girl in my class—a girl I'd been secretly comparing myself to for months. My chest felt like it was caving in and my heart was crushed. I tried to shove down my tears and pretend I wasn't upset, but the damage had been done. The belief that I didn't get the part because my body "wasn't good enough" was set in place.

After that day, my relationship with dancing was no longer fun or enjoyable.

Even though I felt conflicted with my body and with my identity as a dancer, I continued to go to classes four to five times per week. I danced all throughout high school and even considered pursuing dance as a secondary study in college. It wasn't until I auditioned for a college-level dance program that I finally realized the competition was eating me up inside. After I walked out of one particularly challenging audition, I told my mom, "I don't want to do this anymore, I'm done." I stopped taking dance classes and shifted my attention toward my academic education instead.

Over the next few years, the only times I danced was when I was drunk at a party or high on drugs at a music festival. I remember feeling so free and alive when dancing in these environments, but when I wasn't on any substances, I felt self-conscious and awkward in my body. My strained relationship with dancing and my body continued until after my divorce, when I felt called to make my way back into a dance studio. This time, however, it wasn't the traditional dance environment I was used to. My Soul guided me to a new, Feminine, and very edgy dance experience: pole dancing.

When I arrived for my first class, I found myself in a dimly lit studio feeling the energy of excitement and nervousness all at the same time. Looking around the room, I saw women whose bodies were a variety of shapes and sizes wearing very little clothing. When the music began, the teacher guided us to connect with our breath and drop into our bodies. The choreography was sensual, slow, and erotic. Before I knew it, my whole body felt turned on and alive. I watched myself in the mirror as my body flowed through the different movements, and for the first time I glimpsed what it might be like to feel sexy and confident in my body. I also felt the joy and freedom I'd experienced while dancing as a young girl. About halfway through the class, I thought to myself, "Where has this been all my adult life? This is what I've been missing!"

I wish I could say that, from this moment forward, my relationship with my body and dancing completely changed. But it took a few more years before I was truly ready to immerse myself in the world of Feminine movement and embodiment.

After four years of being a student and teacher of mindset empowerment work, I got the itch to go deeper into healing and self-discovery through my body. As I looked around at the Feminine leaders in my industry, I noticed that a select few women were embodying a certain depth of authenticity and self-expression that I felt drawn to. I observed these women as deeply connected to their creativity, their pleasure, and their Feminine magnetism. I watched as they courageously and unapologetically expressed their sensuality, their boldness, and their unconventional beliefs. I could tell they weren't trying to perform or impress anyone; they were simply giving themselves permission to be their authentic selves and allowing their Feminine essence to pour through them. Whatever flavor of personal growth they were tasting, I recognized, was what I was missing.

So, I got curious about what was so different about these women. How were they able to release their fears about what others thought of them, and become more of themselves? The common thread, I discovered, was a practice, lifestyle, and way of being known as Feminine Embodiment.

While I'd heard the term "embodiment" before, it didn't fully resonate until this point on my journey. I'd reached a place where my life, business, and relationships were all going well, yet I was at a plateau with my inner healing. I was craving more aliveness, more pleasure, and more joy. Synchronistically, at this time, I came across a Feminine Embodiment certification program that was being taught by a woman whom I admired and respected. They say that when the student is ready, the teacher will appear, and in this case that couldn't have been more true. Clearly, this was my invitation to say yes to my next level of Feminine exploration.

Over the next ten months, I became a student of Feminine Embodiment work. Through this modality, I uncovered parts of myself that had been suppressed since my childhood and teenage years. I released anger, shame, and unprocessed emotions that had been blocking my authentic expression. And in doing so, I reconnected with my playfulness, sensuality, and personal power. I came back to the part of myself that loved to dance and express herself without a care in the world. I remembered who I was before all of the toxic Masculine programming about being too curvy, too emotional, and too promiscuous took away my joy. My journey of Feminine Embodiment guided me back home to the real me, which not only enhanced my ability to connect more deeply with myself but also opened me up to deeper levels of intimacy in my relationships, more access to pleasure in my body, and greater levels of abundance in my business. I learned what it meant to embrace all parts of myself: the beautiful, the messy, the sensitive, and everything in between.

At the beginning of my Embodiment journey, I never could have imagined the felt sense of what it would be like to live as an Embodied Woman.

I remember asking my teacher: "What if I don't ever get it? What if I never figure out this whole 'Embodiment' thing?"

A big smile spread across her face as she replied, "You don't have to figure anything out. You are already embodied. This practice is about turning up the volume of who you truly are."

Looking back, I have a little laugh to myself, as these questions were clearly coming from a Masculine framework of trying to "figure out the solution." What I know now is that you can't think your way into embodiment; it's something that can only be felt and experienced.

I like to think of mindset work as the Masculine approach to healing and transformation, and embodiment as the Feminine approach to healing and transformation. We need both of them. I also see embodiment as a more advanced and deeper layer of personal growth that can only take place once you have the foundational mindset in place.

In this chapter, we'll explore various modalities to help you deepen your connection with your Feminine body and further awaken your authentic self.

What is Feminine Embodiment?

Feminine Embodiment is a concept that entails feeling more deeply present and connected to the emotions, sensations, and energy that are moving through your body. It can also be described as a practice of:

1. Relating to life through your body,
2. Showing up as your most authentic self, and
3. Living in alignment with your Higher Self

Many people become disembodied due to a history of sexual and/or religious trauma which causes them to unconsciously disassociate from their body, or develop negative body image and body dysmorphia, or patterns of numbing, distracting, and addiction. The truth is, we're never taught how to connect intimately with our bodies, or what it feels like to live inside of our bodies. The irony is that the feelings we seek with our minds—like peace, happiness, contentment, love, and fulfillment—already exist within the body, and can only ever be felt to the depth that we're able to access and connect to the sensations within our bodies.

In Western culture, when we talk about our bodies, we're usually referring to our physical bodies. However, in addition to our physical bodies, which are made up of our organs, bones, muscles, tendons, and skin, we also have access to three other important layers of being: our Energetic, Mental, and Emotional bodies.

The Energetic Body is responsible for your life force energy and your vitality. When energy is stuck or stagnant in your body, it can contribute to dysfunction in both the physical and emotional body. Conversely, blocks in the energetic body can be caused by imbalances in your physical, mental, and/or emotional bodies.

The Mental Body consists of the thoughts that are constantly happening in your mind. It's said that women have between 60,000–80,000 thoughts per day. The quality of your mental landscape (aka your thoughts) influences your stress levels, physical well-being, and emotions.

The Emotional Body is the connection between your physical and mental body. Your Emotional Body consists of all the feelings you experience throughout any given day, week, or month. Your emotions are often triggered by external circumstances/events and have a direct impact on your relationships, health, career, and how you relate to the world around you.

The more attuned you become to the subtle messages of your physical, Energetic, Mental, and Emotional bodies, the more you can consciously enhance how you feel within yourself, relate to others, and perform throughout your day.

Your body is always speaking to you through sensations and emotions. When you experience sensations such as pain, discomfort, tightness, heaviness, or fatigue, your body is signaling that something is out of balance and you need to pay deeper attention to come back into alignment. As we learned in the Emotional Alchemy chapter, if you're feeling sadness, anger, anxiety, grief, or frustration, your body is signaling that something is off and that underlying emotions need to be addressed.

It's only when you start relating to life through the body rather than the mind that you can experience the fullness of life, and start to create a life that's in alignment with your Soul rather than your Ego. As an Embodied Woman, you'll experience the benefits of cultivating a more loving relationship with your body, feeling more connected to your emotions, enjoying more pleasure and aliveness in your body, and living in alignment with your authentic self.

Relating to Life Through the Body

The Feminine body is a wildly intelligent organism. Within the body lives your nervous system, your heart, and your womb. Your body is a sacred vessel for your Soul. While the mind contains Masculine knowledge, your body contains deep Feminine wisdom. Your body allows you to feel sensations and emotions, and to respond to the world from a place of intuitive guidance. Your body always knows what's best for you. It's always speaking to you. It's always guiding you.

When you start living from a place of embodiment, you become connected to the pulse of life itself. Shifting out of the mind and into the body is a continuous daily practice. After decades of responding to life from the mind, it takes time and intention to come back home to your body and to stay connected to Her throughout your day.

There are several different modalities that can support the process of releasing the mind and reconnecting with the body, including intuitive movement practices, yoga, and breathwork techniques. However, not all teachers or expressions of these modalities focus on embodiment, so you'll need to be discerning in selecting teachers and practices.

Yoga as an Embodiment Practice

Perhaps the most well-known practice to facilitate mind-body connection is the ancient practice of yoga. Through focusing on the breath and linking it to movement during a traditional yoga asana practice, we can learn to quiet the mind and create space for deeper connection with the Soul.

Some yoga teachers focus more on the Masculine physical practice of yoga, placing more emphasis on the technical aspects of the physical postures, whereas others help to bring your awareness to the subtle sensations that you experience throughout the practice. The latter is a more Feminine approach that will support you in becoming more attuned to your body and shifting your focus out of your mind and into your body.

Breathwork as an Embodiment Practice

Breathwork (also referred to as *pranayama* in Sanskrit, with *prana* meaning "vital life force and *yama* meaning "to gain control") is a powerful practice to help you go beyond the mind and connect more deeply with your body. Breathwork entails specific breathing patterns and techniques to facilitate an altered state of consciousness and a deeper connection to your energetic and emotional bodies. More intense breathwork techniques such as Holotropic Breathwork—a therapeutic style of breathwork that's done with a trained practitioner—can also facilitate deep emotional releases in which stuck energy, emotion, and/or trauma are released from the body.

As a starting practice, you can play with different pranayama breathing patterns before your morning meditation, between meetings, or before you go to sleep. Whenever you find yourself with a busy mind, you can consciously shift the pattern of your breath to bring you back into the body.

Here are a few different breathing patterns to try:

Conscious Body Breathing

This simple pranayama technique is about bringing conscious awareness to the connection between your breath and your body.

Sit in a comfortable position with your back straight, or lie down on your back. Start to bring awareness to the natural flow of your breath. Gently slow down your breathing to make your inhales and exhales slow and smooth. As you focus on your breathing, bring your awareness to the sensations in your body. On the inhale, notice where you feel the expansion in your body—perhaps in your belly, between your ribs, or in your chest—and on the exhale, notice how everything relaxes and softens.

Continue to trace your breath with your awareness for ten breaths, or until you feel calmer and more relaxed.

4-5-7 Breathing Pattern

The focus of this pattern is about making your exhale longer than your inhale to calm the nervous system and settle anxiety. For this breath pattern, find a comfortable place to sit with a straight spine. Breathe in through your nose for a count of four, pause at the top of the inhale for a count of five, and exhale for a count of seven. Repeat five to ten rounds or until you feel your anxiety dissipate.

Box Breathing

Sometimes it can be helpful to incorporate a visualization while you're doing a breathing practice—in this case, you can trace the shape of a box (or square) in your mind while you follow the breathing pattern. Box breathing is a four-part breath pattern where you breathe in through your nose for a count of four, hold your breath for a count of four, exhale for a count of four, and pause for a count of four.

These are just a few of many breathing practices you can explore to cultivate a deeper mind-body connection. If you feel called to other techniques such as "breath of fire" or "alternate nostril breathing," my suggestion is to explore those in yoga classes or with a trained breathwork practitioner before incorporating them into your home practice.

Ecstatic Dance as an Embodiment Practice

While there are various practices of intuitive movement to explore, ecstatic dance has become an accessible and popular modality. Ecstatic dance is a meditative movement practice in which you can learn how to connect more deeply with your body, emotions, and self-expression.

The founder of the original 5Rhythms ecstatic dance practice, Gabrielle Roth, describes it as a Soul journey, and says, "If you want to give birth to your true self, you are going to have to dig deep down into that body of yours and let your soul howl. Sometimes you have to take a leap of faith and trust that if you turn off your head, your feet will take you where you need to go."[15]

Ecstatic dance, when practiced in a shared community space, is a powerful opportunity to play with self-expression—through movement and sound—the parts of yourself that you may be afraid to share in your everyday life. For me, ecstatic dance has been a deeply healing and cathartic experience in which I've been able to tap into the full spectrum of my emotions, ranging from deep grief to total bliss.

Mirror Dancing as an Embodiment Practice

Mirror dancing is a powerful tool to create a positive relationship with your body, increase your self-love, and become more fully embodied. When you move your body in front of a mirror and intentionally pay attention to what your mind is saying, you can see where there's room for improvement with your inner self-talk.

Traditionally, mirror work is practiced while standing in front of a mirror with or without clothes, and saying positive affirmations to yourself while gazing into your own eyes. Mirror dancing is similar, though instead of standing still in front of the mirror, you're moving your body in an intuitive way that feels good to you.

Mirror Dancing Practice

Here's a step-by-step process for a simple mirror dancing practice:

1. Turn on some music that you enjoy dancing to.
2. Stand in front of the mirror with as little clothing as you feel comfortable with—this could be in a robe, a bathing suit, lingerie, or naked.
3. Look into your eyes in the mirror and take three slow breaths to connect with your body.

4. Start moving your body in any way that feels good to you. Allow your body to move freely, letting go of the need for your movement to look perfect or pretty. If it feels good, you can trace your fingertips or your hands around your body while you're moving.
5. Notice what thoughts or feelings come up for you while you're dancing. If your inner critic comes up to comment on a part of your body you don't like, or if you're focusing too much on how your movement looks, take a deep breath and come back to noticing the sensations in your body.
6. Try dancing to at least one song per day until you get more comfortable with this practice. Eventually, you can dedicate ten to twenty minutes per day to your embodied movement either in front of the mirror or anywhere in your house where you feel free to move as your sensual, empowered, and erotic self.

You'll also find a guided version of this practice at www.amynatalieco.com/bookresources.

Holly's Embodiment Journey

Holly is a successful entrepreneur who came to me because she wanted to learn how to connect more with her Feminine energy. During the day, she was constantly in her Masculine energy and had a hard time turning it off outside of work. She shared that she wanted to deepen her intuition and experience more Feminine flow, pleasure, and ease in her life. Because she was used to being in her CEO role, leading her team at work, and striving to reach the next goal in her business, she felt super disconnected from her body and found it hard to unwind.

At first, when I presented the Feminine concepts of slowing down, creating more space in her calendar for relaxation, and adopting a daily sensual movement practice, she experienced a ton of resistance. Her mind told her: "This is stupid," "This is unproductive," and asked, "Is this even going to work?" But she knew she was unhappy in her marriage and wasn't enjoying her life, so she was committed to making a change.

One of the sensual movement assignments I gave her was mirror dancing. Every day, in the middle of the afternoon, she would take a break from her computer, turn on some music, and dance in front of the mirror. The first time she did this, she felt uncomfortable and awkward. However, with a little encouragement, she kept showing up to the practice, and within a few sessions of mirror dancing she noticed that it felt good to move her hips and allow her body to move freely with the music. Before long, her five-minute mirror dancing sessions turned into thirty minutes of sensual movement and a self-pleasure practice. Her resistance melted, and Holly started to look forward to her daily mirror dancing sessions. She noticed that this practice completely shifted her energy for the rest of the day, helping her to feel less stressed with work, more present with her daughter, and more confident with her sensuality.

By the time we finished working together, Holly had embodied each of the Feminine principles, which allowed her to soften into her Feminine essence and enjoy her life, while still running a profitable and thriving business.

Showing Up as Your Most Authentic Self

After completing a Feminine Embodiment session, I often hear women tell me: "I feel like I've come home to myself; this is the *real* me." When we go beyond the mind, where our limitations, fears, doubts, and insecurities live, we can access the parts of ourselves that are confident, creative, and powerful.

Underneath the stories and conditioning you learned when you were growing up lives the truest, most authentic version of you. You can think of this version of you as your Soul or your Higher Self. When you're living as your Higher Self, you no longer need to conform to norms or expectations. You no longer need to play the "Good Girl" role that your society, family, or religion expects of you. Instead, you can live freely as a fully expressed woman who is unapologetically herself.

When there's a gap between who you truly are inside and who you're pretending to be in the world, it contributes to an internal dissonance that's confusing and painful for your

Soul. Without the masks and facades, people can get to know the real you, and the world can experience your true magic.

Tapping into Your Authentic Self by Embodying Feminine Archetypes

Working with Feminine archetypes is a powerful way to connect with your authentic self and recognize different parts of your true nature that have been suppressed or rejected.

Feminine archetypes were used by psychoanalyst Dr. Carl Jung as a method for self-awareness and healing. Here, we'll focus on five primary Feminine archetypes that are represented in the collective consciousness. Each of these archetypes is classified by a particular set of traits that can be used to awaken and reflect various aspects of the psyche. Additionally, each archetype has a shadow side which represents the darker aspects of human behavior. This shadow side can become present when the archetypal energies are used unconsciously or inappropriately. Therefore, it's important to be aware of both the empowering traits as well as the shadow traits when exploring archetype work.

In the following sections, we'll become familiar with the essence and shadow of each archetype, and learn how to embody the essence of these archetypes in your everyday life.

The Maiden/Little Girl

The Maiden is innocent and naive. She represents the little girl inside each and every woman who was naturally playful, curious, and enthusiastic. Her intentions are innocent and pure, and she's not afraid to express her emotions. Over time, you may have become disconnected from your inner Maiden—either because you were forced to grow up too quickly, or when the responsibilities and challenges of adulthood stripped away your lighthearted and playful side. Even if you've forgotten what it's like to be carefree and to freely express yourself, you can consciously reconnect with this part of yourself as an adult woman.

While some people perceive the Maiden as powerless or weak, that's not the case at all. In contrast to the Masculine tendencies to strive, achieve, accomplish, and progress, the Maiden's naivety and innocence demonstrate the power of joyful, unstructured play for play's sake. The Maiden reminds us of a time when there was nothing we needed to accomplish, no milestone we must hit, and no reason to feel embarrassed for being our authentic selves. The Maiden invites adult women to soften into our vulnerability and invite more child-like wonder and play into our lives.

When the Maiden is out of balance or in her shadow expression, she can come across as needy, flighty, or overly attached. She can also get stuck in "Good Girl" programming where she's a people pleaser, perfectionist, and strict rule-follower. She may seem helpless, codependent, and overwhelmed by the responsibilities of the world around her. The key is to notice when these shadow aspects are present and to attend to any childhood wounds or patterns that are contributing to these behaviors.

You may choose to embody the Maiden when you notice you've been taking life too seriously or when you've become overly structured in your life. Another powerful place to call upon the Maiden is when you notice emotions or triggers arising throughout your day. By connecting to the Maiden archetype, you can bring compassion and empathy to your inner child or the part of you that didn't feel safe to express her emotions when you were younger.

Ways to embody the Maiden:

- Incorporate playful activities: dancing, hula hoop, playing games.
- Bring curiosity into your daily tasks and projects.
- Wear something colorful, sparkly and/or unique.
- Try a new hobby or explore a new creative outlet.

The Mother/Caregiver

The Mother is the giver of unconditional love and compassion. She's nurturing, caring, generous, and gentle. The Mother offers wisdom, guidance, comfort, and safety to those in her care. Additionally, she's the symbol of fertility and creation for all of life.

In Western culture, the Mother is often depicted as a martyr who sacrifices her own needs and desires to take care of others. Women today often have a complicated relationship to the Mother archetype, whether because of the stereotypes and expectations surrounding motherhood, or because of the complex relationships they've experienced with their own mothers. However, the Mother archetype is not just about bringing children into the world and raising them with kindness; rather, she represents a woman who prioritizes care and creation in all of its forms. In order to care for others, she must first care for herself, and develop strong boundaries so that she can give to others from a full cup.

When the Mother is out of balance or in her shadow expression, she can be overbearing, controlling, manipulative, and codependent. When her children or creations are threatened, she can be vengeful, spiteful, and defensive. When she feels unneeded, unwanted, or useless, she may be closed off to protect her heart. Ironically, this can cause the Mother to give even more, trying to prove that she's valuable and needed. If you notice that the shadow side of the Mother is present for you, bring awareness and self-compassion to this pattern and come back to focusing on self-care, setting healthy boundaries, and focusing on your own happiness.

You can call upon the Mother archetype when you're feeling depleted, or you notice that you could use more nurturing and support. You can also call upon her to self-soothe and to offer yourself compassion when you have challenging emotions or negative self-talk arising.

Ways to embody the Mother:

- Focusing on self-care: take a bath, get some rest, cook a nourishing meal.
- Spend time in nature to connect with Mother Earth (aka the Great Mother).
- Offer yourself words of compassion when you're feeling sad, scared, and/or overwhelmed.
- Birth your ideas and creative projects into the world.

The Lover/Seductress

The Lover is sensual, confident, and playful. She's deeply connected to her emotions and exhibits a magnetic quality wherever she goes. The Lover enjoys intimate connections with others in both physical and emotional forms. She's all about sensuality, connection, and pleasure in every sense of the word. She luxuriates in every sensation she experiences throughout her day, taking in the textures, flavors, colors, sounds, and aromas of life.

While some may misunderstand the Lover as being promiscuous, "slutty," or irresponsible with her sexual energy, the Lover is a very natural expression that each of us contain as Feminine beings. Rather than being reckless and careless, the Lover is intentional about whom she shares her energy and heart with.

When the Lover is out of balance or in her shadow expression, she can be dramatic, overly indulgent, manipulative, or have addictive tendencies. When she fears abandonment, or becomes dependent on chasing pleasure without connection, she may feel disconnected from herself and ungrounded. Without a deep sense of self-worth, she may become dependent on external validation to feel safe or happy.

You may call upon the Lover when you find that you've been overthinking, overworking, or when you feel like you need more connection with others.

Ways to embody the Lover:

- Giving yourself a sensual massage.
- Wearing lingerie around your house, just because.
- Slow, sensual Feminine movement, focusing on moving your hips in circular motions.
- Wearing soft clothing, touching a soft blanket, or laying on a soft rug.
- Creating space to honor your emotions through journaling or expressing your feelings with a lover, partner, or friend.

The Wild Woman/Huntress

The Wild Woman archetype can be characterized as unapologetic, untamed, and fierce. She's empowered, direct, bold, and determined. The Wild Woman is devoted to truth above everything else. She speaks what's in her heart, stands firmly in her boundaries, and holds her standards high. Contrary to the "Good Girl" persona, the Wild Woman is unafraid to be messy in her emotions and to express her authentic self. She stands up for what she believes in, and advocates for herself and others when she experiences or witnesses injustice.

Some people feel intimidated by the Wild Woman because she's fully expressed and living in her true power. They might think that she's "too intense," "bitchy," or "out of control." These are just projections and judgments based on how society has taught women to behave. The Wild Woman doesn't care what other people think of her. She shows up as herself, knowing that the people who resonate with her will be magnetized toward her, and the people who are triggered by her will fall away (or come back at a later date).

When the Wild Woman is out of balance or in her shadow side, she can be chaotic, destructive, and unpredictable. If you start to notice that you're exhibiting these traits, check in with yourself to see where you're feeling suppressed, judgmental, or overwhelmed. Slow down and get curious about whether you've been playing small, or if there are any areas of your life where you're not upkeeping your boundaries or speaking your truth.

Ways to embody the Wild Woman:

- Setting boundaries in your relationships.
- Leaning into conflict, using your voice, and speaking your truth with fierce love.
- Exercising to feel strong and empowered in your body.

- Expressing yourself through dance, song, drumming, or other creative practices.
- Sacred rage practices to release anger or frustration.

The Queen/Ruler

The Queen is confident, worthy, and devoted. She's loyal and protective, a heart-centered leader. Her energy is centered in trust, integrity, and a deep sense of loyalty. The Queen has high standards and calls other people forward into their greatness. Rather than using her power to suppress or control, the Queen seeks out the best in others and empowers them to use their gifts to contribute to the collective. Although she has a deep sense of ambition and confidence in her own capabilities, the Queen is open to asking for, and receiving, support, and is willing to outsource and delegate to others.

From watching fairy tales and movies at a young age, many of us learned to see Queens as evil women who are self-centered, demeaning, and controlling. It's true that, when the Queen is in her shadow expression, she can be shallow, manipulative, materialistic, and judgmental. She can become fixated on gaining power, feeling possessive of everything she's accumulated, and unwilling to let others in. She may use her influence to fulfill insecure needs, rather than those for the greater good. She may doubt herself or become mistrustful of others.

Even when the Queen is in her benefic expression of the mature, wise leader, many may be intimated by her, and turn their own sense of inferiority into a judgment against her. Our society in general tends to vilify powerful women.

You can call upon the Queen when you want to feel more confident within yourself and connected to your greater vision. Any time you want to step into greater leadership or be of service to others, the Queen will help you overcome self-doubt and remind you of your inner power.

Ways to embody the Queen:

- Get clear on your vision for your life and how you want to show up in leadership.
- Make clear decisions and take action toward your dreams.
- Pay attention to other people's gifts and acknowledge them for their talents.
- Outsource tasks and allow others to support you.
- Take the lead on a project or bring people together in community.

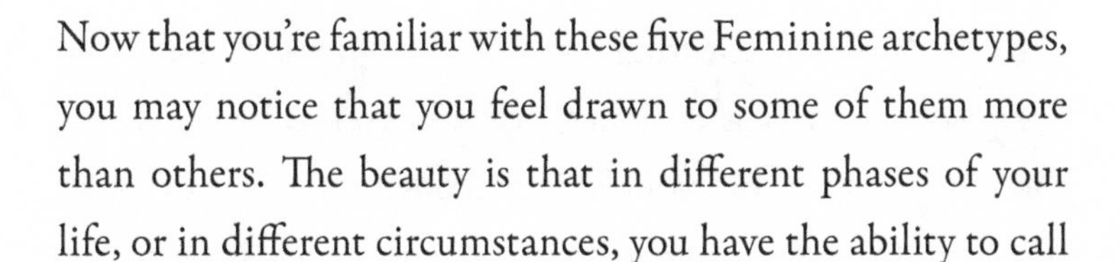

Now that you're familiar with these five Feminine archetypes, you may notice that you feel drawn to some of them more than others. The beauty is that in different phases of your life, or in different circumstances, you have the ability to call upon whichever archetype(s) feel most supportive for you. By understanding the traits and the shadows of each archetype, you may start to notice that you're already exhibiting some of the characteristics from each of them. Or you may recognize areas for improvement that inspire you to work more deeply with a specific archetype.

There's no right or wrong way to work with archetypes. You will be intuitively guided toward whichever archetype is going to serve you the most. Remember, the whole point in working with these archetypes is to become the most fully expressed and empowered version of yourself. In addition to the embodiment practices provided in each archetype description above, you can also connect more deeply with each archetype through the practices of visualization and intuitive movement. What would it feel like to move through your day as the Queen? The Mother? The Wild Woman? Try it out and see for yourself!

Embodying the Feminine Archetypes Through Intuitive Movement

Another way to practice embodying the essence of these archetypes is to bring them into an intuitive movement practice. Begin by selecting music that helps you tap into the energy of the particular archetype you're connecting with. As the music plays, close your eyes and connect with how your body would move, and perhaps even what sounds you might make if you were embodying that archetypal essence fully. Think of it as dancing with the energy of the archetype, or preparing for a role as this archetype in a movie or play. What are the characteristics and personality traits you can bring forward? For example, if you're connecting with the Maiden archetype, what type of music would you listen to and how would you express playfulness, innocence, or joy through your movement?

At first, this practice may seem strange, uncomfortable, and even silly. However, the deeper you allow yourself to go into this practice, the easier it will be to access the archetypal traits you wish to embody in your everyday life.

If you're new to this practice, it may feel easier to be guided by a practitioner until you feel comfortable doing it on your own. You can download a free embodiment session at www.amynatalieco.com/bookresources. Additionally, you can find great embodiment teachers to work with in person through my mentor Nadia Munla's website (www.embodyby-nadia.com) or through a well-known Feminine Embodiment company called S Factor.

Living in Alignment with Your Authentic Self

When you're living as an Embodied Woman, there's no gap or separation between who you are and how you're acting or behaving. You're living in alignment with your values, walking your talk, and showing up as the powerful Feminine leader you came here to be.

On an energetic level, other people can feel when you're living in alignment with your values. Unfortunately, there are many people who say that they believe in love, integrity, and health, but when you peel back the curtain and see how they really act, there's an incongruence with how they portray themselves and how they actually show up in their lives every day. When you're walking your talk and being who you portray yourself to be, people feel safe and trust you more.

In the beginning stages of any personal development path, it's common to feel a disconnect between the version of yourself you have been up until now and the version of yourself you're becoming. You can think of the identity that you're stepping into as your "Higher Self," which is ultimately who you already are at your core. The only difference between this version of you and who you are right now is that your Higher Self shows up in her true nature regardless of the limiting beliefs, insecurities, and negative self-talk that were previously keeping you small.

Embodying Your Future Self Visualization

The first step to aligning with your Higher Self is to connect with Her through an embodied visualization practice like the one in this section.

This exercise has three parts, which I've separated for the sake of clarity. Feel free to return to this exercise any time you want to connect with your future self. You can also listen to the audio version of this visualization at www.amynatalieco.com/bookresources.

Step One: Visualize

- Drop into a quiet, meditative space.
- Take a few deep breaths to connect with your body and quiet your mind.
- Bring to mind a visual of your future self—a version of you that's one to five years older than you are now.
- Connect with how this version of you looks and how she feels. Is she powerful? Confident? Courageous? Radiant? Relaxed? Healthy? What is she wearing? How does she carry herself?
- Get curious about how this version of yourself moves throughout the world. How does she speak? How does she act? How does she speak to herself and to others?
- Imagine what it feels like to be this version of yourself. Feel these sensations in your body. With every breath, let them get brighter and louder. Allow these sensations to seep into every cell in your body.
- Take a moment to notice any shifts that you're feeling in your energy and in your body.
- Come back to your breath for a few more minutes and allow this feeling to settle inside of you.
- When you're ready, open your eyes and write in your journal to reflect on what you felt and what you saw.

Step Two: Release

Once you've completed your future self visualization and journaling practice, it's time to get clear on how to close the gap between who you are today and who you are becoming. Remember, this process is not about becoming like someone else or completely changing who you are, but rather about releasing any Ego-based constructs and patterns that have been covering up who you truly are at your core.

With that said, the next step in this exploration is to identify any beliefs, thoughts, and habits not in alignment with your Higher Self. As you go through this exercise, be sure to do so through the lens of curiosity instead of being judgmental and hard on yourself. Remember, you are human, and we all have patterns that we've developed over time that contribute to undesirable behaviors and decisions.

Some examples of what you may need to release:

- Self-criticism and negative self-talk.
- Feeling like you don't have enough value to offer.
- Not trusting yourself to make decisions.
- Settling for less than you deserve.
- Saying yes to commitments even when you want to say no.
- Putting your self-care and spiritual practices on the backburner.
- Perpetuating codependent patterns in your relationships.

- Relying on alcohol and other substances for stress relief.
- Going to sleep too late and/or snoozing your alarm clock.
- Getting distracted on your phone and spending too much time on social media.

Once you're clear on the top three to five patterns you wish to release, write them down on a piece of paper. You can then do a simple release ceremony where you burn the paper or rip it up into pieces and energetically let go of what is no longer serving you.

From now on, every time these patterns come to the surface, take a moment to honor whatever feelings of frustration, guilt, or shame are present, take a deep breath, and ask yourself, "What choice would my Higher Self make here?" Then move forward in that direction. Even if you do go back to the old thought pattern or habit, give yourself grace and remember that you can always choose again tomorrow. It's through having grace and compassion for yourself that you'll be able to successfully change these ingrained patterns and beliefs.

Step Three: Align

The final step toward living in alignment with your Higher Self is to get curious about what thoughts and habits your Higher Self would implement into her daily life. When you connect with the future version of yourself that you're becoming, ask yourself:

- How would she start her day?
- How would she talk to herself?
- How would she take care of her body?
- How would she value her time?
- How would she navigate challenges when they arise?
- How would she communicate her needs and desires?
- How would she interact with other people?

Select one to three new thoughts or habits that you can start to implement into your life on a daily basis. It's important that you don't try to implement too many changes at once, because that often leads to overwhelm and makes the changes more difficult to maintain in the long run. Once you feel like you've successfully implemented one or more new habits or beliefs, come back to your list and pick another one to work with. Soon you'll be living in greater alignment with your Higher Self every day.

Now that we've explored a variety of different perspectives on what it means to be an Embodied Woman, and covered several modalities to connect with your authentic self, it's time to apply this wisdom to your everyday life.

One simple way to infuse the principle of Feminine Embodiment into your lifestyle is through adding embodiment practices to your existing morning or evening rituals. Another way is to pay attention throughout your day when you're feeling disembodied, and take a few moments to bring your energy and focus back into your body. As a refresher, some of the simple practices you can return to throughout your day are: intentionally connecting to your breath, taking a dance or intuitive movement break, and slowing down to check in with your body and emotions to see what you need to feel more balanced.

The more you incorporate these embodiment practices, the easier it will be for you to recognize when you're feeling disembodied, and the faster you'll be able to return to an embodied state. For example, before I understood what it felt like to be disembodied, I would get to the end of my workday with my body feeling tense and exhausted. After learning what it feels like to live from my body instead of constantly being in my mind, I started to become more attuned to what my body needed throughout the day to stay calm, energized, and relaxed. Similarly, the more I experienced what it felt like to be my authentic self, the faster I was able to notice when I was being inauthentic or suppressing my emotions. You'll know that you're living as an Embodied Woman when you feel confident and relaxed in your body and free to be your authentic self no matter who you're interacting with.

The beautiful thing about embodiment is that it's an ever-unfolding journey of meeting and expressing new parts of yourself. In doing so, you'll increase your capacity to flow with the waves that life brings your way, and begin to effortlessly see how your external reality shifts to align with your desires and dreams. As an Embodied Woman, you'll not only notice shifts in your own life but also start to see how other people are inspired and transformed simply by being in your presence.

In our final chapter, we'll explore how to use the principle of Feminine Embodiment to step into your role as a Feminine leader during this time of the Feminine Rising.

Soul Reflections

- What is your current relationship with your body? Is it loving? Kind? Challenging? Resentful?
- Write a love letter to your body thanking her for all of the ways she's supported you and allowed you to experience your life. After you're done, reflect on how writing this changed your perspective on your body.
- Which Feminine archetype(s) do you feel called to embody more of in your life? What qualities does she have that you wish to awaken or strengthen within yourself?
- Describe what your life will look and feel like when you fully embody your authentic self.

"The Divine Feminine encourages interdependence, interconnectedness, and mutual support."

Layne Redmond

chapter ten

Integrating the Feminine Codes

As we've explored throughout our journey together, living in The Feminine Way is not about being in your Feminine energy all the time. Instead, it's about learning how to come back into harmony with the Masculine and Feminine energies that live inside of you. This return to inner union is a process of unlearning our old ways of operating, reconnecting with your empowered Feminine essence, and learning how to dance between these two energies in your everyday life.

When you begin awakening your Feminine energy after it's been dormant or suppressed for too long, you might find yourself swinging to the other end of the polarity pendulum and operating too heavily in your Feminine energy. This pendulum swing is not bad or wrong; sometimes it's necessary to explore the edges of polarity in order to find your own unique harmony and flow. You'll know that you're too far in your

Feminine energy if you're feeling ungrounded, unclear, or unproductive to the extent where you feel anxious about your lack of forward movement or you find yourself dropping the ball on important commitments. When this happens, implementing some Masculine structure can be helpful to come back into balance.

When I realized that I was feeling burnt out and exhausted from functioning in Masculine overdrive in my business, I swung super far into the Feminine realms. This was the same period in my life where my intuition guided me to put my belongings in storage and start my nomadic journey. For the next eight months, I resisted having *any* structure in my life and my business. I booked one-way plane tickets to each new destination and was flying by the seat of my pants in my business without any strategy or goals. My inner free spirit and rebellious nature was coming out to play, and my Soul was craving an immense amount of freedom without restriction.

For about six months, I experienced the most amount of liberation, pleasure, and aliveness I'd felt in my entire life. Even though I didn't have a game plan in my business, I still attracted amazing clients—with a lot less effort—and was able to financially support myself while I traveled around the world. You could say that I was living the entrepreneurial dream, and it definitely felt like I was living my best life. But eventually, I started to crave more stability and structure. After months of traveling, I felt an inner yearning to set roots down and find a home base for myself. Even though my business was doing well, I knew that if I wanted to scale to the next level of success—from an aligned and sustainable way—then I would need to implement new strategies and have more clarity in my direction.

After settling into my new home in Asheville, North Carolina, I started to come back into equilibrium and find a more balanced flow between my Masculine and Feminine energies. While there were times when I still found myself swinging too far from one end of the pendulum to the other, I learned how to recognize when the imbalance was happening and consciously choose to come back to my center. The more I practiced this dance and gave myself grace when it wasn't perfect, the more natural it became for me to flow between the two. From this place of embodied polarity, I've seen more stability, success, and expansion in my business, while experiencing more fun, ease, fulfillment, and joy in the other areas of my life.

In this chapter, we'll be reviewing the Seven Feminine Codes from the perspective of harmonizing our Masculine and Feminine energies and creating effortless flow between the two. This authentic, alchemical mixture of Masculine and Feminine will help you tap into your Higher Self and create the future you envision.

A Feminine Approach to Evolution

As you've been learning throughout this book, the Feminine approach to healing and growth is one of nurturing, compassion, and self-love. When learning a whole new way of being and relating to life, it can be helpful to take the Buddhist mindfulness approach of having a beginner's mind. Instead of having high expectations of "getting it right," or feeling like you "should be better at this already," the Feminine invitation is to approach this journey from a place of patience and curiosity.

Along your journey, there will inevitably be times where you fall back into old patterns like overworking, overdoing, and prioritizing goal-oriented actions over your daily rituals. This doesn't mean that you're moving backward, or that you haven't made any progress. It simply means you're human, and that you're learning and growing.

The Feminine teaches us that growth is cyclical. Similar to our own cyclical nature that we covered in Chapter Eight, your growth trajectory is not always meant to be trending upward in a linear, Masculine fashion. I think about spiritual healing as peeling back the layers of an onion to get to the core of who you are. For this reason, it's inevitable to revisit old fears, patterns, and habits along the way. It's often through experiencing the contrast of coming back to old patterns and behaviors that we're reminded why it's so important for us to stay on the path.

If—or should I say when—you find yourself reverting to old patterns, you can either view this experience from a place of self-criticism and shame, or you can see it through the lens of compassion and self-love. It may seem counterintuitive to bring yourself compassion when you're not showing up in the way you want to. However, you've probably already learned from experience that being hard on yourself doesn't really get you anywhere. It's through compassion and forgiveness that you can come back to a place of empowerment and make better choices moving forward.

Nora's Integration Journey

Nora is a high-performing, well-educated, and successful finance professional. She's one of only a few female partners in the firm where she works, having worked her way up to one of the top positions in her company. After graduating from Harvard Business school and pursuing her career path, she found herself feeling dissatisfied with her personal life and deeply desiring a romantic relationship.

Leading up to our time together, she'd worked with several nutritionists and personal trainers but kept finding herself back in the same place with emotional eating patterns and regaining the weight she lost whenever she went on a diet. Up until this point, she'd unconsciously been taking a hyper-Masculine approach in every area of her life, including her career, weight loss journey, relationships, and day-to-day lifestyle. It's no wonder she felt bloated, exhausted, and like something was missing.

As we started our work together, we focused on customizing the Feminine Codes in a way that she could integrate them into her current work schedule and lifestyle. Over time, she became more consistent with her daily rituals and her self-care practices. Her relationship with her body went from being one of frustration and discomfort to one of self-love and respect. Instead of using food to numb her emotions, she learned how to address her emotions in healthy ways. Through this approach, Nora lost weight without going on a diet and felt more confident in her body than ever before.

About a year into our work together, Nora went through a stressful time at work. There were some big changes happening that would potentially require her to move to a new city. On top of this, she'd been talking to a man that she was interested in and felt disappointed when things didn't come to fruition in the way she'd hoped. During this emotional time, she noticed that she'd reverted back to old patterns of overeating, skipping her morning practices, and not taking care of herself. Once again, she found herself bloated, gaining weight, and feeling overwhelmed with stress. In the past, this would have led to a downward spiral where she would gain more weight and go back to her old ways. But this time was different.

Rather than letting her inner critic take over, she practiced bringing compassion to herself and got curious about what was contributing to her feeling out of alignment. She worked with the Emotional Alchemy code to release the deeper emotions of frustration, fear, and anxiety that were causing her self-sabotaging behaviors. Then she recommitted to her daily devotion rituals and everything else fell back into place. As she reconnected with her Feminine energy, her stress levels came back down and she reprioritized her health and reconnected to her intuition. Through aligning with the Feminine Codes, she gained the clarity and courage to take the new job opportunity and move to a new city to advance in her career, all the while continuing to honor her Feminine flow.

Letting Go of the Destination

When we take a high-pressure Masculine approach to change, we can become hyper-focused on getting to our final destination above all else. While there are times when having an end goal and a clear timeline is helpful—such as training for a marathon or completing a certification—applying the same approach to your Feminine awakening journey will not serve you in the same way. Rather than thinking of this process as having an end destination or a finish line, it can be helpful to view it as an unfolding journey that will continue to evolve over time.

As you move through different chapters and seasons of your life, you'll continue to discover new parts of yourself and have opportunities to deepen your connection with your Feminine energy. Additionally, different chapters and seasons of your journey may require you to focus on specific Feminine Codes more than others. For example, if you're going through a breakup, you may focus on alchemizing your emotions or honoring your cyclical nature. Whereas if you're going through a career change, you might focus on awakening your intuition or connecting with your Soul Calling.

If you notice yourself feeling like you should be further along, remind yourself that this isn't a race. You're always exactly where you're supposed to be on your journey. And if you keep showing up in daily devotion to your unfolding, you'll receive exactly what you need in perfect timing. If you notice that something is feeling out of alignment or that you're not heading in the direction you want to go, come back to your daily devotion practices and check in with your intuition for guidance.

It really is that simple. The hardest part is trusting the process.

After supporting hundreds of women through this process, I know it can be easy to fall into the comparison trap, feeling like you should be doing more or getting better results based on what you see other women doing. This is just your Ego feeding you the illusion that other people are better than you. The truth is that we all have our own timeline of awakening, and we all experience challenges along the way. When you notice yourself getting stuck in comparison, take a step back to reset and return into your own lane. If you need to unfollow other women on social media or take a break from looking at what other people are doing, that is totally okay. Remember that comparison is never the key to getting the results you want. Instead, take time to reflect on how far you've come, acknowledge all of the effort you have put in so far, and get curious about ways you can continue to move forward from a place of self-love and confidence.

Finding Your Own Structure and Flow

When I first started exploring my inner dance of Masculine and Feminine polarity, my approach was more calculated than intuitive. As I transitioned out of Masculine overdrive, I was able to use some of the healthy Masculine skills I'd become really good at, such as planning, structure, and organization to make more room for my Feminine flow.

In the beginning, I scheduled times in my calendar on a daily, weekly, and monthly basis to be in my Feminine energy. This helped me remember and prioritize my Feminine practices. Each day, I blocked off thirty minutes in the morning, a thirty-minute break for lunch, and a ten-minute segment in the afternoon to connect with my body through dancing, going for a walk, stretching, or intentional breathing. Each week, I scheduled one or two yoga classes, two evenings to get out in nature or watch a sunset, and made at least one "sister date" with a girlfriend. I also added the new and full moon dates to my calendar, and tracked the start dates for my menstrual cycle.

Without these reminders in my calendar, it would have been easy for me to keep going on autopilot and get to the end of each day without tuning in to my Feminine energy. Of course, even though I had reminders, there were times that I ignored the notifications and kept plowing through whatever tasks I was doing. When this happened, I would give myself grace and compassion, and choose a different time that day or week to come back to whatever I'd skipped. After a while, this process became more intuitive; I began to notice where

I was pushing too hard and allowed my body, emotions, and energy to guide me back into harmony. In the past, it took getting to the point of exhaustion, being emotionally reactive, or having a headache to recognize when I'd swung too far in my Masculine energy, but as I became more attuned, present, and embodied, I was able to notice subtle cues before I reached the tipping point. Taking a break became something I chose versus something I was forced to do when I'd reached depletion. Similarly, whenever I found myself spending too much time in my Feminine flow, I was able to recognize when it was time to shift gears and activate my Masculine energy to bring more structure, focus, and momentum.

As you move through your own Feminine awakening, you'll find the unique balance of structure and flow that works best for you. Remember that during different chapters of your life you may need to prioritize your Masculine or Feminine energy more. This isn't a rigid or calculated process. It's a living and breathing unfolding as you dance throughout different seasons of your life.

Practical Tools for Finding Balance with Masculine and Feminine Polarity

The Feminine Codes we've covered throughout this book are designed to support you in living a life that's pleasurable, fulfilling, and nourishing. Living in alignment with The Feminine Way is the answer to reclaiming your aliveness, radiance, and vitality.

Once you've learned how to reconnect with your Feminine energy, the journey forward is about continuing to navigate the dance between your inner Masculine and Feminine on a moment-by-moment basis. By intentionally infusing more Feminine energy into your life, you'll find that your relationship with life itself will radically transform. From this place of rebalancing your energetic state, you'll start to see changes in every aspect of your external reality—including, but not limited to, your health, relationships, career, and lifestyle.

Let's explore what energetic harmony looks like in each of those areas.

Polarity with Your Health

In the old paradigm, we're taught to ignore the warnings of our physical and emotional symptoms. It's considered normal and acceptable to override these signals so we can stay on track with our goals and continue to uphold the image of success through our external image and social status. As we've discussed throughout this book, The Feminine Way is about slowing down and listening to our mental, emotional, and physical cues. As we pay attention to and honor our bodies' messages, we can take the necessary steps to decrease physical stress, tend to any physical pain, and take care of our immune systems. This level of care, nourishment, and attunement allows us to work in harmony with our bodies so we can experience greater energy and vitality, as well as identify health issues before they get out of control. When we're operating at this high vibrational frequency, we not only feel better on all levels but we're also able to show up in a greater capacity for our relationships and our Soul Calling to create positive change in the world.

Polarity in Female Relationships

As human beings, relationships are a fundamental aspect of our survival and our emotional well-being. We're social-emotional creatures that require connection and love in order to thrive. More specifically, as women we're community-oriented because historically we needed each other to raise children and tend to the village when the men were out hunting or fighting battles.

The further we've ventured into the patriarchal, Masculine way of living, the more isolated and shut down we've become toward connecting authentically with others. Living in The Feminine Way is about dropping into the heart and softening into vulnerability in your relationships. Connecting with your Feminine heart-space awakens feelings of forgiveness, compassion, and grace. As you connect more deeply with your Feminine essence, you become open to a whole new level of emotional depth and connection in your romantic and platonic relationships.

As I've shared, prior to implementing the Codes of The Feminine Way, I had a really challenging time connecting with other women. I struggled with comparison, competition, resentment, and jealousy. It wasn't until I went through my divorce and finally started living as my authentic self that I began attracting Soul-aligned friendships with other women in my life. This unique bond, which I experienced for the first time in my life in my late twenties, is what I now refer to as "true sisterhood." The more deeply I connected with my Feminine essence and focused on my own inner healing, the easier it became for me to open my heart to other women. At this point in my life, sisterhood has become one of my greatest joys and highest values—something I cherish above all else. The level of connection and support I receive through my intimate female friendships offers a richness and stability in my life that I didn't even know existed before.

Later in this chapter, I'll show you how to begin healing your sisterhood wounds, start creating authentic connections with other women, and call in your Soul sisters.

Polarity in Romantic Relationships

Now that you have the tools to bring awareness to your Feminine energy, you can intentionally cultivate more polarity in your romantic relationships.

If you notice that the chemistry has decreased in your partnership, you now have the tools and awareness to drop into your Feminine energy through your Embodiment, Soul alignment, and Emotional Alchemy practices. As discussed in Chapter Six, taking a few minutes at the end of your day to shift from your Masculine to your Feminine energy can drastically shift your experience by allowing your partner to step more into their Masculine energy. If you notice that this shift isn't happening, treat it as an opportunity to share with your partner what you've been working on, and communicate your desire for them to actively step into their Masculine energy in your romantic relationship.

Now you might be wondering, "Do I always have to be in my Feminine in my relationship?" The answer is no. You have the freedom to flow between your Masculine and Feminine energies based on what works best for you and your romantic partner. There may be times when it feels better for you to take the lead (both inside and outside of the bedroom), and other times when it feels better for your partner to take the lead. Assuming the Feminine role in your relationship doesn't mean you need to be "submissive" to your partner or give up your power. In fact, as you've learned in this book, the Feminine is incredibly powerful and sensual! Instead, it's about showing up to your relationship from a place of openness, receptiveness, vulnerability, and feeling connected to your body.

For some heterosexual couples, it's possible to experience chemistry when a woman is in her Masculine energy and when a man is in his Feminine energy, as well as the other way around. For same-sex or gender-fluid couples, one partner may naturally fall into a more Feminine role, or the dance may be unique and deliberate from day to day. There is no one recipe for what works, and the process of discovery can be both fun and exciting.

Polarity in Your Work Life

As you infuse more Feminine energy into your work life, you will find that you feel more energized, fulfilled, and alive throughout your day. Instead of being in "hustle" mode all the time, you'll know when it's time to focus and be productive, and when it's time to drop into rest and take a break. Your body will be the greatest guide during this process.

If you notice that you're tired, anxious, or have physical tension in your body, these are signs for you to pause and ask, "What do I need to do to take care of myself right now?" Alternatively, if you notice that you feel energized, creative, and inspired, this is a sign to direct your energy toward the projects and tasks that you're working on to maximize your output. What you will find is that, rather than working longer hours or pushing harder, you'll be more productive, focused, and inspired, which will allow you to work less while still making progress.

In different seasons of your business—for example, when you're launching a new program or when it's a busier season in your industry—you may need to spend more time in your Masculine energy. However, even if you're in a busy season, make sure you're still honoring your Feminine energy by staying devoted to your morning rituals, taking movement breaks, and remembering to breathe and slow down throughout the day. You may need to be more intentional about your social engagements and other commitments so that you have time to rest outside of your workday as well. You can also honor your Feminine by building in several days of "down time" after the busy period wraps up so that you can recover your energy and get the rest you need.

Connecting with your Feminine energy in your work life will also help you to tap into your innate magnetism and ability to receive. Instead of having to force or push to get results, you'll start to notice a sense of ease with new opportunities coming your way.

Polarity in Your Lifestyle

Bringing Feminine energy to your lifestyle means feeling more in flow with life. Rather than getting overwhelmed by your to-do list, you'll find that you're able to flow between your "doing" energy and "being" energy with ease. Even when you're going through a chaotic time in your life—such as the holiday season, preparing for a wedding, becoming a parent, or having a ton of social commitments, you'll find that you're able to prioritize pockets of time to reconnect with yourself and soften into your Feminine energy. You'll still likely have some seasons that feel busier than others, but instead of feeling like you're falling behind or not getting enough done, you'll start to trust in the natural cycles of life and know that everything is unfolding perfectly as it's supposed to.

On a day-to-day basis, it will become easier to intuitively listen to your body and pay attention to your energy levels, hunger levels, and emotions to determine what you need in each given moment. As you do this, you'll find that you're able to trust yourself more, and that you feel less of a need to control your external environment because you feel in harmony within yourself. Soon your external reality will start to reflect your internal harmony. You'll experience less resistance from negative people and challenging situations, and be far less triggered when resistance does arise because you know how to regulate your internal state.

Building in Accountability and Support

Now that you've received the wisdom of The Feminine Way, it's time to take action and continue to integrate this methodology into your life. As I mentioned before, this is an ongoing journey and there will be many twists, turns, and challenges that come up along the way. From my own experience working with hundreds of clients over the years, there are a few key elements that I've found to be incredibly supportive when it comes to ongoing transformation and integrating The Feminine Way into your life.

Community and Sisterhood

Being on the path of Feminine awakening is not an easy journey. It takes tremendous courage to be willing to do things differently than the status quo and to dive deep into the depths of your inner healing. For this reason, going through the cycles of healing on your own can feel lonely and isolating. It can often feel like no one understands what you're going through, which can make this process feel confusing and scary.

The truth is that we're not meant to go through this awakening on our own. Women have gathered together in community to support one another since the dawn of civilization—yet, over time, we've lost touch with this sacred practice of coming together in sisterhood. Instead, we've taken the wounded Feminine energies of competition and jealousy and infused them into our relationships with other women. Despite what we've been told, this is not our natural way of relating to one another.

We've all seen the "Mean Girl" archetype portrayed in movies, and most of us had experiences growing up where we felt hurt or rejected by other women. These painful experiences cause us to develop "sisterhood wounds." We feel like we cannot trust other women and are therefore scared to open up for fear of getting hurt again. Underneath this learned programming, we all have a desire for authentic connections with other women. We all want to feel seen, heard, loved, and understood.

There are many incredible healing benefits available when you allow yourself to be seen and supported in sisterhood. Back in 2019, I hosted monthly in-person women's circles as part of my community called New Moon Collective. Through these monthly gatherings, I witnessed an immense amount of healing through women coming together in a safe and supportive environment to share what was on their hearts and to be witnessed and celebrated by other women.

Through various intimacy exercises, women would share things about themselves that they were too afraid to share with other people in their lives. In doing so, they realized that they weren't the only ones who'd struggled with depression, anxiety, or unresolved trauma. Through being seen and heard by other women, the shame that they had been carrying around a specific experience or part of themselves would quickly dissolve.

Another aspect that I loved witnessing in these spaces was the way that women were able to reflect to one another their natural power and beauty. Sometimes it can be challenging to see ourselves the way that other people see us, but when another woman is willing to share the light and strength they see in you, it can help you to see these parts of yourself more clearly.

When you surround yourself with empowered, embodied women, you'll find that you're inspired to become the best version of yourself. Through observing other women's success and growth, your vision for yourself will continue to expand and you'll start to believe in yourself in a whole new capacity.

So, how can you find women to whom you can relate on this deep, authentic level?

The first step to cultivating authentic sisterhood in your life is to focus on healing your relationship with yourself. When you work through your own insecurities and past wounding, you'll develop a deeper sense of self-love and inner confidence. This will support you in feeling less triggered by (and to be more open to) other women. In order to receive sisterhood love, you need to be prepared to hold that pure space for others.

In addition to developing deeper self-love, start to pay attention to any of the stories of comparison, judgment, and competition that come up during your interactions with other women. When you notice these toxic patterns, take some time to reflect in your journal about where these patterns may have originated. Did you learn this way of thinking from your mom, or from witnessing older women gossip when you were growing up? Did you have an experience where you felt hurt or disappointed by another woman that led to you feeling like you can't trust women? Were you in a Masculine work, school, or sports environment that taught you to be competitive with others? Once you know where these patterns come from, you can start to release these old beliefs and choose new beliefs that are more in alignment with how you want to live your life moving forward.

Next, you'll want to get clear on how you want your relationships with other women to feel, and what values are most important to you when it comes to your friendships. Do you want your friendships to feel nourishing, supportive, and energizing? Do you want your friendships to be mutually giving, honest, and consistent? Do you want to feel like you can be your full self around these women? What types of activities and experiences do you want to share with these women? Describe the dream friendships that you're calling in.

Lastly, it's time to take action. In order to meet new people who are more aligned with the version of yourself that you're becoming, you have to be courageous and put yourself out there. This could look like trying a new yoga or fitness studio, going to local personal development workshops, or joining a women's circle. Essentially, you'll want to put yourself in spaces where other growth-oriented women are gathering. I've met some of my best friends through participating in group coaching programs and masterminds, attending seminars, and going on spiritual retreats.

If you don't have access to any women's groups in your area, there are plenty of online communities to explore. One great place to start is the Global Sisterhood (www.globalsisterhood.org) or Sistership Circle (www.sistershipcircle.com). Additionally, if you have a desire for these types of gatherings but they don't exist yet in your local area, this could be an opportunity to take the lead and create something yourself.

Remember that it can take time to get to know people and to form deeper connections. So, if you feel like you want to pursue a friendship with someone you've met at a gathering or an event, it's up to you to take the initiative and start the conversation. Don't sit back and expect the relationship to blossom on its own; friendships need to be watered and nourished in order to grow over time. As you put in the effort to nurture your budding sisterhood connections, pay attention to see if you're feeling met by the other person (or people) with their energy and communication. It's okay to be discerning about which relationships, communities, and groups you pour your time and energy into. It's totally normal to not feel fully aligned with or to not feel connected to every single person or community. Everyone you meet has something unique to teach you, but while some friendships are meant to last a lifetime, others are meant to last only a season.

As you continue to evolve and grow, people will flow in and out of your life. This goes for both old friendships and new ones. As you open to your Feminine energy, you may find that even some of your lifelong relationships no longer feel nourishing or aligned for who you're becoming. For example, you may find that some old friendships feel superficial, and you're craving deeper intimacy and connection. Or perhaps your current friend group is partying excessively or engaging in "Mean Girl" behaviors that no longer feel good in your body. When this happens, it can feel challenging, confusing, and scary to let these relationships go. However, the sooner you're willing to surrender relationships that are no longer meant for you, the less painful the process will be, and the sooner you will call in new relationships or deepen existing ones that are truly aligned. Throughout my own journey, I've had several painful friendships transitions that felt similar to going through a romantic breakup. I've learned—through using my Emotional Alchemy practices—how to navigate these transitions better, and how to come back to a place of love and gratitude for the friendship we shared, even when it wasn't meant to continue.

The more you continue to show up as your authentic self, the easier it will be to attract aligned friendships into your life, and to discern which spaces and communities will best contribute to your growth. Trust the process, and don't allow yourself to settle for relationships that don't bring you joy, connection, and ease.

Coaching and Mentorship

One of the fastest ways to grow is to surround yourself with people who've already embodied the results and success you want to achieve in your life. At the beginning stages of your Feminine awakening journey, you likely have been focused on self-study through reading books (like this one), listening to podcasts (like my Feminine Frequency podcast), or by exploring various classes and workshops. As you take in this knowledge and wisdom, you'll notice that you have a greater awareness of your patterns and behaviors that haven't been working for you, and start to shift some of your beliefs and habits based on what you're learning.

While self-study is a great first step, there may come a point on your journey where you have a lot of awareness but still feel stuck in repeating hyper-Masculine patterns or like you can't get out of your own way. Or perhaps you've made a ton of progress, but you desire to access your next level of success more efficiently and effectively. If you find yourself in either of these scenarios, this is a great time to look for a coach or mentor who can guide you through a deeper healing and transformation process.

As humans, we often want to figure things out on our own and resist asking for support. Especially as women, it can be hard to open up to receive support from others. However, a skilled mentor, guide, or coach can support you by creating a Masculine structure so that you can be fully in your Feminine energy of receiving. Instead of trying to figure it all out and hold your emotions all on your own, you now have someone to lean on for support, and who can walk side by side with you on your healing journey.

Another powerful benefit to coaching is that skilled coaches can help you identify your "blind spots," meaning unhelpful patterns and blocks that you aren't able to see on your own. Often, when we're in our own minds, living our own lives, it can be hard to see the deeper patterns hiding in our subconscious mind. It takes someone who can ask the right questions and offer honest reflection to help us see what's standing in the way of our authentic expansion.

Additionally, as you move through your growth journey, there will be times where you need to be reminded of your self-worth and supported to reconnect with your greater vision. A good coach will remind you of the truth, and believe in you when you forget to believe in yourself.

Remember, no matter what coach or mentor you choose to work with, it's not their role to "fix," heal, or change you. Instead, their role is to support and guide you so that you take back your Feminine power and make those changes for yourself.

If you're curious to find out more about the in-depth coaching programs I offer in my coaching practice, visit www.amynatalieco.com

Retreats, Seminars, and Workshops

These are great opportunities to learn about the wide range of modalities that exist to support your inner healing journey and Feminine Embodiment. These offerings are more experiential and immersive than books, podcasts, or your own daily rituals. There's also a deeper level of healing available when you take a break from your home environment and surround yourself with other inspiring, growth-oriented people in a curated container.

Something truly magical happens when women (and men) gather together with the shared intention of inner healing and connecting with a like-minded community. My client, Jenn, after attending a four-day retreat, said: "I came in as one version of myself and left as a different woman." If you've never been on a retreat or taken time out of your busy schedule to specifically focus on your personal growth through seminars or workshops, I highly recommend that you find an experience that feels aligned for you to attend. If in-person events aren't possible for you right now, there are many online workshops and even multi-day retreats available.

Now that we've explored the Seven Feminine Codes and covered various ways to integrate them into your life, it's time to choose your action steps. It's likely that you've already started to notice some shifts in your energy and perspective through reading this book and completing the Soul Reflections at the end of each chapter. However, the real integration begins when you set this book down and begin to move through your life with this new knowledge of The Feminine Way.

Remember, embodying The Feminine Way is not about "doing" more, but rather about becoming the empowered and fully expressed woman that your Soul came here to be at this point in history. Your embodiment is the key to creating positive change and transformation for all living beings, for our planet, and for future generations. This is the true power of The Feminine Way, and the deeper reason for incorporating this work into your everyday life.

Soul Reflections

- In which areas of your life do you feel there's more room for integration between your Masculine and Feminine energies?
- How do you feel about your current relationships with other women?
- Describe how you want your relationships with other women to feel?
- What are some action steps you can take to meet other like-minded women?

Afterword

The warm breeze washes over my skin as I listen to birds chirping all around me in the tropical jungle of Costa Rica. As I write this final message to you, I can't help but feel a sense of awe and gratitude for how The Feminine Way has led me to the path I'm on today. In this moment, my body is filled with aliveness, creativity is flowing through me, and I feel surrendered to the flow of life. I attribute this state of being to my daily devotion to the Divine Feminine over the past six years.

And, while I know that my life has been completely transformed through cultivating inner harmony between my own Masculine and Feminine energies, I'm also aware that this way of living is an ongoing practice that I'll continue to be in relationship with for the rest of my life. As I continue to show up for my daily devotion practices, listen to my intuition, honor my emotions, prioritize pleasure, align with my cycles, and live in my Soul Calling, I continue to discover deeper layers of my authentic self and learn new ways to live as a fully Embodied Woman. Rather than waking up feeling depressed, depleted, and disconnected from myself, I now find myself living a life beyond my wildest dreams—and it just keeps getting better.

When I open my eyes in the morning, I see natural lighting streaming through my windows and Feminine beauty all around me. I feel blessed to live in a home sanctuary that feels peaceful and inspiring. My heart overflows when I think about the quality of the relationships I have with my Soul sisters, my Soul brothers, and my community. I'm experiencing more pleasure, love, and intimacy than ever before in my romantic partnership. I prioritize time in nature, dance, play, and connection on a regular basis. Every day, I show up as my authentic self and feel excited about what I'm creating in my life and my business. As challenges arise, I turn to my Emotional Alchemy and Embodiment practices to navigate any fears that surface and come back to a place of joy and radiance. My life is filled with an abundance of love, money, support, and pleasure. Most importantly, I feel a deep trust in God(dess), the Universe, and life itself. I'm in a state of deep surrender for whatever life has in store for me, and I feel excited for the magic that lies in the unknown. My ability to flow between my Masculine and Feminine energy in my life, business, and relationships allows me to feel at ease as I show up consistently to align with the greater vision for my happiness and success.

Not only has The Feminine Way positively transformed all aspects of *my* life, but it's also transformed the lives of thousands of students, readers, and podcast listeners around the world. I've seen lives radically change as a result of this work. That's how I know that all of what I've just described, and more, is available to you as well, starting today.

During this era of great healing and transformation, the people who choose to align with a more conscious way of living will continue to thrive and evolve in a direction that enhances their life experience. Alternatively, those who choose to cling on to the old paradigm, allow fear to take over, and continue operating in the outdated, imbalanced, hyper-Masculine structures will experience great resistance and struggle. Without balance, life cannot flow; we need both the riverbed and the water flowing through it.

On a larger scale, when more leaders embrace The Feminine Way, all aspects of humanity will be positively impacted—including, but not limited to: our romantic and platonic relationships; our physical, emotional, and social well-being; and the regeneration of the earth (aka the Great Mother). Heart-centered leaders within organizations and politics will initiate and influence new, more positive social, governmental, corporate, and environmental structures. This elevation in consciousness will ripple into future generations, in which young women and men will navigate the world with more love, peace, balance, and strength than ever before. With the power of the Feminine within us, we'll change the world.

It's a true honor and blessing to be living in the time of the Feminine Rising. I see women (and men) all around the world awakening to the Divine Feminine wisdom that's here to transform and heal the trajectory of humanity and the planet. As we discussed in the initial chapters of this book, the collective transformation that's underway starts with each individual doing their own inner work to align with a new belief system and way of living. As each woman awakens, she gives other women permission to live in their truth and create a life within the new paradigm of vitality, pleasure, and fulfillment.

If every woman were to live her life in alignment with The Feminine Way, they would be able to contribute to their families, communities, and society from an overflowing cup. Through implementing and embodying the Feminine principles in this book, you'll regain your health, pleasure, and aliveness. As you refuel your radiance, power, and vitality, you'll be able to share your wisdom and your gifts to the world in a larger capacity on a consistent basis. And in return, you'll receive an abundance of love, freedom, and money to support you in creating a life beyond what your mind can currently imagine. You'll develop a deep sense of self-trust, faith, and confidence.

As you show up more and more as your fully embodied self, without holding back your voice, creativity, and authentic expression, the people around you will feel uplifted and inspired by your presence. Each time you listen to your intuition and make a courageous decision, you'll develop a deeper level of self-trust and confidence, and you'll no longer rely on external ideas or opinions to guide your life's path. You'll find the courage to pursue work that you're passionate about that feels fulfilling and aligned with your Soul gifts. You'll begin to attract relationships that are mutually supportive and inspiring where you feel unconditionally seen, heard, and appreciated. And you'll be surrounded by women who celebrate, respect, and support you through the good times and the challenging ones as well.

My wish for you, dear reader, is that you take the wisdom you've received through this book and infuse it into every aspect of your life. As you show up in daily devotion to your practices, be gentle with yourself, and remember that this journey is not about "getting it right." Embracing imperfection and having compassion for yourself along the way is the key to continued growth and expansion. Even when life feels chaotic and stormy, come back to your daily devotion rituals, tune into the wisdom of your body, and you'll find peace and clarity within.

Now is the time to go forth and live as the Embodied Feminine leader that your Soul came here to be in this lifetime.

With love and devotion,
Amy

resources

You'll find additional meditations and resources to continue integrating the Feminine Codes into your life at: www.amynatalieco.com/bookresources.

Subscribe to the Feminine Frequency podcast on Spotify, iTunes, or Apple Podcast to access a library of over 300 podcast episodes that are devoted to The Feminine Way.

To explore guided meditations and spiritual courses, download the Insight Timer app at www.insighttimer.com

For guided breathwork practices, download the Pause Breathwork app at www.pausebreathwork.com/app

For self-pleasure tools such as crystal wands and yoni eggs, visit www.waands.com or www.yonipleasurepalace.com

To support menstrual cycle tracking, download the Flo App www.flo.health or the MyFLo Period Tracker at www.floliving.com/app

For women's circles and sisterhood support, visit www.globalsisterhood.org or www.sistershipcircle.com

To find a local embodiment teacher and/or to become a certified embodiment teacher, visit www.embodybynadia.com or www.sfactor.com

endnotes

1. Majo Molfino, *Break the Good Girl Myth: How to Dismantle Outdated Rules, Unleash Your Power, and Design a More Purposeful Life*, HarperOne, July 2020
2. Londin Angel Winters and Justin Patrick Pierce, *The Awakened Woman's Guide to Everlasting Love*, Sacred Existence, February 2018, p.151
3. Dr. Bradley Nelson, *The Emotion Code: How to Release Your Trapped Emotions for Abundant Health, Love, and Happiness*, St. Martin's Essentials, May 2019
4. Dr. Robert Plutchik's Wheel of Emotions: www.positivepsychology.com/emotion-wheel
5. Emily Nagoski, *Come As You Are: The Surprising New Science that Will Transform Your Sex Life*, Simon & Schuster, March 2015
6. www.deloitte.com/global/en/about/people/social-responsibility/women-at-work-global-outlook.html
7. www.cdc.gov/violenceprevention/pdf/2015data-brief508.pdf
8. www.pubmed.ncbi.nlm.nih.gov/28213723
9. www.pleasurebetter.com/orgasm-statistics

10. Sheri Winston, *Women's Anatomy of Arousal: Secret Maps to Buried Pleasure*, Mango Garden Press, January 2010
11. www.rebeccacampbell.me/oracledeck
12. www.positivepsychology.com/what-is-flow
13. www.sciencedirect.com/science/article/pii/S1550830719305476
14. www.risingwoman.com
15. Gabrielle Roth, *Sweat Your Prayers: The Five Rhythms of the Soul – Movement as Spiritual Practice*, Tarcher Perigee, December 1998

acknowledgments

I would like to express my deepest gratitude to the following beautiful Souls who contributed to *The Feminine Way* coming to life.

Bryna, Marie, and the whole team at WorldChangers Media, who guided me through the technical and emotional process of writing, editing, and publishing my first book. Without you, this book would still be a dream living in my heart. Thank you for your belief in me, your belief in my vision, and your support every single step along the way.

Mom, Dad, and Ricky for your unconditional love and support as I continue to embody my authentic self and follow the path of my Soul. Thank you for sticking with me through the good times and the challenges along the way.

Johnny Blackburn for being an incredible mentor and guide during the darkest times of my spiritual awakening. Thank you for being the embodiment of healthy Masculinity and for lovingly witnessing my evolution into the woman that I am today.

Kayote Joseph for being my first spiritual mentor and a living embodiment of what it means to be a fully expressed and empowered woman. Thank you for teaching me that I have the power to create the life of my dreams.

Nadia Munla for guiding me on my own Feminine Embodiment journey and teaching me how to facilitate embodied transformation for other women. Thank you for being the powerful, embodied, Feminine woman and leader that you are.

Jessika Schonberg for being my best friend, confidante, and Soul sister for life. There are no words to describe the depth of your friendship and the ways that you've supported me over the years. Thank you for being a cheerleader for this book writing process and for believing in me.

Corey Duvall for being my partner, my greatest supporter, and my deepest love. Thank you for seeing me through the eyes of unconditional love and for celebrating my Soul mission in this lifetime.

Scout Sobel for being a dear Soul client, colleague, friend, and inspiration. Thank you for trusting me to be your mentor and for sharing my work with your community. Thank you for leading the way and showing me that it was possible for me to become an author.

To my Soul clients whom I've had the honor and privilege to mentor and learn from over these past six years, thank you for showing up to do your inner work and for being part of the ripple effect of embodied transformation.

And finally, Feminine Frequency podcast listeners for tuning in week after week and sharing the impact that this Feminine wisdom has had on your lives. You're my inspiration for writing this book. Thank you, thank you, thank you.

about the author

Amy Natalie Pamensky is a Women's Empowerment Coach and Feminine Embodiment Guide with over a decade of coaching experience. She specializes in helping women to emerge as the most authentic, confident, and self-expressed versions of themselves.

Her mission is to ignite women into their Feminine power so that they can live a life of freedom, pleasure, fulfillment, and purpose.

As a community leader, Amy creates transformational spaces for women to experience radical healing and deep Soul connection through retreats, workshops, events, and group coaching programs.

Amy is also the host of the Feminine Frequency podcast, which at the time of this writing has over 500,000 downloads and 300 episodes, and reaches women from all around the globe.

Visit Amy's website www.amynatalieco.com to learn about her group coaching, online courses, private mentorship, events, and retreats.

about the publisher

Founded in 2021 by Bryna Haynes, WorldChangers Media is a boutique publishing company focused on "Ideas for Impact." We know that great books change lives, topple outdated paradigms, and build movements. Our commitment is to deliver superior-quality transformational nonfiction by, and for, the next generation of thought leaders.

Ready to write and publish your thought leadership book with us? Learn more at www.WorldChangers.Media.

Printed in the USA
CPSIA information can be obtained
at www.ICGtesting.com
JSHW021604141223
53812JS00007B/44